# LOYAL HEARTS

## HISTORIES OF AMERICAN
## CIVIL WAR CANINES

# LOYAL HEARTS

## HISTORIES OF AMERICAN
## CIVIL WAR CANINES

By Michael Zucchero

*Michael Zucchero*

Foreword by Patrick A. Schroeder

SCHROEDER PUBLICATIONS

2009

**Front Cover:** "The Mascot," 2007, John Weiss, licensed courtesy
of The Greenwich Workshop, Inc., www.greenwichworkshop.com

Published by
SCHROEDER PUBLICATIONS
131 Tanglewood Drive
Lynchburg, VA  24502
www.civilwar-books.com
civilwarbooks@yahoo.com

Printed by
McNaughton & Gunn, Inc.
Saline, Michigan

ISBN-1-889246-57-3

*In memory of my mother, Jane Zucchero, who truly loved dogs and would have loved this book.*

*And to my retrievers Hershey and Randy, with whom I made the long march.*

A dapper looking corporal sporting a non-commissioned officer's sword is accompanied by a little friend of dubious origin. The breed of this dog could be a Cockapoo. *(Author's Collection)*

# Table of Contents

# Photo Index

# The Dog of the Regiment

"If I were a poet, like you, my friend,"
Said a bronzed old Sergeant, speaking to me,
"I would make a rhyme on this mastiff here;
For a right good Union dog is he,
Although he was born on 'secesh' soil,
And his master fought in the rebel ranks.
If you'll do it, I'll tell you his history,
And give you in pay, why—a soldier's thanks.

"Well, the way we came across him was this:
We were on the march, and twas getting late
When we reached a farm-house, deserted by all
Save this mastiff here, who stood at the gate.
Thin and gaunt as a wolf was he,
And a piteous whine he gave 'twixt the bars;
But, bless you! If he didn't jump joy
When he saw our flag with the Stripes and Stars.

"Next day, when we started again on the march,
With us went Jack, without word or call,
Stopping for rest at the order to halt,
And taking his rations along with us all,
Never straggling, but keeping his place in line,
Far to the right, and close beside me;
And I don't care where the others is found,
There never was [a] better drilled dog than he.

"He always went with us into the fight,
And the thicker the bullets fell around,
And the louder the rattling musketry rolled,
Louder and fiercer his bark would sound;
And once, when wounded, and left for dead,
After a bloody and desperate fight,
Poor Jack, as faithful as friend can be,
Lay by my side on the field all night.

"And so, when our regiment home returned,
We brought him along with us, as you see;
And Jack and I being much attached,
The boys seemed to think he belonged to me.

And here he has lived with me ever since;
Right pleased with his quarters, too, he seems.
There are no more battles for brave old Jack,
And no more marches except in dreams.

"But the best of all times for the old dog is
When the thunder mutters along the sky.
Then he wakes the echoes around with his bark,
Thinking the enemy surely is nigh.
Now I've told you his history, write [wrote] him a rhyme,
Some day poor Jack in his grave must rest,
And of all the rhymes of this cruel war
Which your brain has made, let his be the best."

Moore, Frank (editor and compiler) *The Civil War in Song and Story,*
P. F. Collier Publisher 1889, 440.

**George Armstrong Custer rests in camp with one of his favorite
dogs at his feet. The dog has apparently been playing fetch in a
wet and muddy area. Custer had a great affinity for dogs and
often took several on campaign with him.** *(Courtesy of the Library
of Congress)*

"The Talking Dog." This canine appears to be saying: "I am the Dog that went through the army with the 28th Iowa Infantry." Stamped on the back: "Capital City Photo Studio by Baldwin & Daugherty, 5th and Walnut Street, Desmoines, IA." *(Author's Collection)*

**A wartime image of Lieutenant Colonel Austin Sprague Cushman, 47th Massachusetts Infantry and his faithful companion.** *(Massachusetts MOLLUS Collection. U. S. Army Military History Institute)*

# Foreword

Soldiers during the American Civil War adopted many exotic mascots. They ranged from alligators to badgers and bear cubs to wildcats, but none were as common, loyal and affectionate as dogs. The total number of canine mascots from the period is not known, but a few attained minor celebrity status and were memorialized on reunion buttons and monuments. In this book, Mike Zucchero tells the famous stories of "Dog Jack," "Harvey," and "Sallie," as well as those of lesser known four-legged friends.

For every documented dog in the field, there were undoubtedly dozens that only lived on in the memories of the soldiers. Yet dogs were active in their military lives: sharing men's trials and tribulations, offering their affection and providing entertainment to soldiers that faced hour upon hour of military boredom or possible death in an instant. Unfortunately, many of these mascots likewise became casualties. The appeal of a dog mascot seems to have overwhelmed some soldiers so much that they took to dognapping. Confederate General Harry Hays' men of the Louisiana Brigade abducted the tiny mascot "Stonewall" from the Richmond Howitzers several times.

At the battle of Sailor's Creek, after fighting around the Lockett Farm and across the Double Bridges, troops of Federal General Andrew Humphreys' Second Corps captured a large portion of the Confederate Army of Northern Virginia's wagon train and found a litter of puppies among the wagons. One of the most famous photographs of the Civil War, taken by Timothy O'Sullivan at Appomattox *(see page 142)*, shows Federal soldiers in front of the Appomattox Courthouse building. This particular photograph is frequently misidentified as being taken in April 1865, when in fact it was taken in the late summer or early fall of 1865 when Company D of the 188th Pennsylvania was posted in the county on Provost Guard duty. Upon enlargement, the photograph reveals two soldiers have small dog mascots in their arms, though one blurred as a result of movement during the long exposure. Although there is no known written documentation of these canines, the photograph indicates 60 men of the Provost Guard had at least two dogs.

The 102nd Pennsylvania Infantry's multiple dog mascots included "Jack" and "York." Early on in the war, as the regiment advanced in line of battle, York patrolled the left flank with Company B while Jack advanced with the right flank. York died from the rigors of campaign life leaving Jack the regimental favorite. As a sign of their high regard for their beloved mascot, the men clubbed together and bought Jack a $75 silver collar at a time when a soldiers' pay was $13 a month. Jack was captured with some of the regiment at the battle of Salem Church, Virginia, on May 3, 1863, and held with them as a prisoner of war at Belle Isle, Virginia, until he was exchanged for a Confederate soldier. Jack disappeared near Frederick City, Maryland, on December 23, 1864, and the men speculated that Jack was killed by robbers for his silver collar. Interestingly enough, there was a second dog named "Jack" of another regiment, the 56th New York Infantry that also received a special collar purchased by the men. This Jack fared better despite being wounded at the battle of Fair Oaks, and survived all the regiment's battles and returned home to die of old age. A third dog named "Jack" or "Union Jack" served with the 1st Maryland Infantry (U. S.).

Federal Civil War photographs of soldiers are far more numerous than photos of Confederates. The same is true for dog mascot images—the lone Confederate dog photo being of "Tinker" who served on the crew of a blockade runner. As far as stories, there is more parity and includes "Frank" of the Orphan Brigade's 2nd Kentucky Infantry (C. S.) that carried his own rations in a haversack specially made for him. Also, the last known dog fatality on the battlefield was "Charlie" of the Georgia Troup Artillery killed in action at the Battle of Cumberland Church, April 7, 1865, only two days before General Lee's surrender.

Zucchero uses his impressive collection of photos, as well as others, and extensive research to include 57 illustrations and create 19 chapters that present the reader with the most extensive work to date on Civil War canines. This fully indexed volume is a valuable resource, an entertaining read and provides a fitting tribute to army dogs of the Civil War. It is sure to please Civil War enthusiast and dog lovers alike.

Patrick Schroeder
Lynchburg, Virginia

14

# Preface

*A REMARKABLE DOG—Nearly every company, certainly every regiment, in the service, has a pet of some kind or other. It matters not whether the object of their affection be dog, cat, possum, cow or horse, whatever it be, the brute is loved by all, and woe be to the outsider who dares to insult or injure one of these pets. More personal encounters have been brought on between soldiers about some pet animal, than in any other way. Occasionally these pets become great heroes, in their way, and then they become general favorites with the whole army.*[†]

Ever since wolves, the common ancestor of today's numerous canine breeds, first wandered into the light of a Neolithic campfire, the history of man and dog has been intertwined. The evolution of the domestic canine has been shaped by the evolution of civilization and (to some extent) vice versa. Thanks to their instincts, dogs have proved useful as faithful companions, guards, hunters and trackers, messengers, detectives, protectors and warriors. It's hardly surprising, therefore, that canines have been key players in one of mankind's most ancient "arts"–warfare.

Though references are sometimes made to American Civil War canines being used as messengers and sentries, I've found little evidence to suggest that most dogs accompanying the men of North and South were "mustered in" for specific functional purposes. To the contrary, the vast majority of dogs seem to have been incidentally attached to particular units or brought to the battlefields by their

---

[†] Stewart, Alexander M. *Camp, March and Battlefield: or Three Years and a Half with the Army of the Potomac.* (Philadelphia: J. B. Rodgers, 1865), 274.

owners. Most Civil War canines were personal pets and company or regimental mascots, not "four-legged soldiers" assigned to specialized duties.

Of course, lack of official rank or specific assignments didn't stop many dogs from taking the initiative themselves. Some canines chased down would-be deserters, awakened slackers, sounded alerts when the enemy was near, guarded prisoners, chased rats aboard navy ships, comforted the wounded, and stayed by dead companions until they could be properly identified and buried. The stories that follow contain instances of incredible canine bravery, compassion and sacrifice.

*Loyal Hearts* isn't just a collection of dog stories. Because the history of man and dog has been mingled for millennia, America's Civil War is the story of both creatures. The lives of these heroic mascots cannot be faithfully document without also capturing the thoughts and experiences of the men who cared for these dogs, and who were similarly cared for by their dogs. The bloodiest conflict in American history cannot be accurately told without the heart-wrenching stories of both the four legged and two legged soldiers who endured it.

In order to maintain the emotion, drama, and poignancy of their first-person accounts, I have made liberal use of direct quotations from the men who actually witnessed the events described in this book.

*Loyal Hearts* tells some of the lesser-known tales related to the American Civil War, but it is far from definitive. Some facts have been lost over the last century and a half, while other information remains silent in collections and local archives. Other details may be hidden in basements and attics throughout the nation. So, while reading this book, if you realize that you possess or know someone who has valuable information about any of the dogs featured in *Loyal Hearts* or any other American Civil War canines, please contact the publisher or send an e-mail to Cwdogs1861@aol.com. This additional information may be used in subsequent editions of this book.

My warmest regards,

Mike Zucchero

# Chapter 1

## Sergeant

Admitted to the Union on August 10, 1821, as a slave state, Missouri was officially neutral at the start of the Civil War. Despite this designation, Missourians were anything but dispassionate observers to the bloody conflict tearing apart their nation and home state. In fact, depending one's point of view, Missouri was either an unofficial member of the Confederate States of America, or a hotbed of Union sympathizers seeking Federal rescue from secessionist Governor Claiborne Fox Jackson.

Missouri witnessed some of the most brutal fighting of 1861. There were two major battles that decided her fate. Battles were soldiers were shot through the body with musket balls or struck down by artillery; thousands of lives were lost, both human and canine. The first battle was called Wilson's Creek by the Union, Oak Hills by the Confederates. It was fought 40 years to the day after Missouri was admitted to the Union.

One regiment that saw action on that day was the 3rd Louisiana Infantry, mustered into state service in April and May, and formally received into Confederate service on May 17, 1861.[1] As more than a thousand of these men marched north, they encountered a dog that would become their beloved mascot, whom they named Sergeant.

The dog joined the regiment in mid-July 1861, near Camp Jackson in northwest Arkansas. A soldier in the 3rd Louisiana, W. H. Tunnard, who later wrote a history of the regiment, described the meeting:

> *When the army first left Camp Jackson on the march, a large dark-and-tan-colored dog attached himself to the regiment, and soon became a universal pet. When on the march he invariably trotted along the road a few paces in advance of the van, hence earned the sobriquet of "Sergeant." He seldom left his position in front of the moving column, when the regiment was ordered out of camp.*[2]

Sergeant dutifully marched with the regiment through pouring rain and intolerable heat. Together, dog and men entered Missouri on July 28. As "a universal pet," Sergeant must have been appreciated for more than the positions he took up along the marches. No doubt, the men fed and cared for Sergeant, probably even pampered him, as some surviving photos attest that many canine mascots were undeniably *very* well fed.

The 3rd Louisiana marched into the southwest corner of Missouri, part of a larger army of 12,000 commanded by Major General Sterling Price, Missouri State Guard, and Brigadier General Ben McCulloch, both veterans of the Mexican War. Along the way, the men received reports that a Union army was heading south to confront them. The Union force, half as strong as the Confederates, was led by another Mexican War veteran, Brigadier General Nathaniel Lyon, along with Major General Samuel D. Sturgis. Though the Union had fewer troops here, they were better equipped than the Confederates. A significant number of the Missourians led by Price had no uniforms, tents or even guns. Others were only equipped with shotguns or antiquated flintlocks. As substitutes for artillery projectiles, they were preparing to fire smooth stones and rusty chains from their ancient cannons.[3]

Sergeant's presence brought welcome relief to those men anticipating their first taste of battle with joy a combination of excitement and dread. With a dog in the regiment, the men had a pleasant distraction from their fears and the tedium that accompanied days of endless marching. On August 10, however, this tedium came to an abrupt and violent end.

Just moments after the sun rose over the eastern horizon, the battle began. The isolated pop-pop of musketry fire was soon augmented by the flash and roar of Federal cannons, the booms shaking men from their slumber. The Confederates were eager to test their mettle against the Union soldiers, but few could have predicted the fearful slaughter awaiting them. Shortly after the first sounds of battle, the 3rd Louisiana was formed up by Colonel Louis Hebert and began advancing toward the enemy's positions. Soon, they came within range of Federal artillery. Tunnard wrote:

> *As the regiment advanced through the dense undergrowth towards the open field, a terrible and scathing fire was opened on them by nearly double their numbers of U. S. Regulars, the flower of General Lyons' army. The regiment rapidly wheeled into line of battle, each company taking its position with prompt celerity. Numbers of the men had already fallen.*[4]

In its first engagement with Union infantry, the regiment suffered many casualties, including its cherished pet, Sergeant. In his book, *A*

*Southern Record*, Tunnard's account of Sergeant is entitled "A Death Not Reported In Official Reports."

> *. . . On the morning of battle of Oak Hills, "Sergeant" was on hand to participate in the events of the day. Amid the storm of leaden bullets and the fierce rattle of musketry in the first close, deadly and obstinate engagement with the enemy, "Sergeant" charged through the bushes, leaping over logs and obstacles, barking furiously all the time. He seemed to enjoy the fight exceedingly. As he passed down the line, his sharp voice attracted the attention of some of the men, one of whom shouted to him, "Get out of that Sergeant, you d—d fool, you'll be killed." The words were scarcely uttered ere a fatal ball struck him, and, with a long piteous whine, he rolled on the ground never to rise. The intelligent animal fell among the prostrate forms of many who had fed and caressed him, the victim of his own fearless temerity.[5]*

Despite Sergeant's death on the field, the men of the 3rd Louisiana continued fighting until 1:30 in the afternoon. Shortly afterward, the battle was over for the 3rd Louisiana, as Union forces retreated toward Springfield. Wilson's Creek was a complete Confederate victory. It was the first major engagement following the Union's defeat at Manassas, Virginia, a thousand miles to the east, and the tide of battle had been nearly identical. Initial Federal gains were halted, repulsed, and then the Confederates routed their Union brethren. But like Manassas, the Confederates were too exhausted by day's end to pursue the enemy to its destruction.

The 3rd Louisiana's losses were 9 killed, 47 wounded, 3 mising[6] and 1 death not reported in the official records, the dark-and-tan dog known as Sergeant.

Another battle, in six months time, fought in northwest Arkansas would decide the fate of Missouri. In April 1862, at the battle of Elkhorn Tavern, the 3rd Louisiana was again part of an army matched against smaller Union forces. But this time, the battle resulted in a decisive defeat for the Southerners. The men of the regiment could not know it then, but Elkhorn Tavern was the Confederate army's last gasp for Missouri. Though guerilla bands continued raids across the state until the war's end, Missouri was effectively secured for the Union from that point.

Missouri received a star on the Confederate flag, but this was little more than hollow symbolism, a tiny swath of fabric that did little to aid the Confederate cause. Missouri was in Union hands forever; just six months after Sergeant gave his life, not for that cause, but for the men in gray and butternut who had lavished their affections on him.

**Written in period ink on the reverse side of this Carte de Visite is "Killed June 2nd 1863." Photographer and dog are unknown, ca. 1860's.** *(Author's Collection)*

**Company A, 8th New York State Militia and mascot in June 1861 at Arlington, Virginia.** *(Courtesy of the Library of Congress)*

# Chapter 2

## A Furry Prisoner of War

During the war, well before opinion pollsters regularly checked the public's political pulse, there was little, if any way to determine what percentage of people favored the Union or Confederate causes in any given region. What is definitely known is that significant numbers of pro- and anti-Union sympathizers could be found in every state, above and below the Mason-Dixon Line. The war was not just *between* the states, but *within* the states. This was especially true in Maryland.

In early May 1861, a recruiting office was opened in Baltimore by Captain John C. McConnell, under the auspices of Colonel John R. Kenly and "other prominent loyal citizens of Maryland." By the end of the month, ten full companies of volunteers enlisted to serve in the 1st Maryland Infantry.[1]

A year later, in one of many ironies that characterized the Civil War, the men of the 1st Maryland Infantry (U. S.) would be opposed by another 1st Maryland regiment, this one fighting for the Confederate States of America. The place was Front Royal, Virginia, in the lush Shenandoah Valley.

The Confederates attacked Front Royal between noon and 1:00 p.m. on May 23, 1862, with a force at least 18 times larger than Colonel Kenly's nine companies of 1st Marylanders, except for Company E, which was guarding a railroad station eight miles east of town. Despite the overwhelming odds, Kenly's men held the enemy for nearly six hours, the resistance ended shortly after Kenly was severely wounded. Although most of Kenly's men were captured, the delay of the Confederate advance allowed Federal General Nathaniel P. Banks to move his division to the Maryland side of the Potomac, saving most of his division from being trapped in Virginia.[2]

Estimates of the number of Union prisoners taken in that action vary, but the number was over 500 men. The 1st Maryland (U. S.) had been beaten and beaten badly, but they remained defiant. As the battle came to a close, they tore their regimental colors to pieces and divided the shreds, rather than let them fall into the hands of the enemy.

*When it became evident that further resistance would avail nothing, and while the enemy was closing around the heroic band, who for six mortal hours had fought to maintain the honor and glory of their country's flag, a rallying cry for the colors went up, and brave hearts hedged it round, presenting a living barrier to the charging cavalry, until, as a last resource, and to prevent its falling into the hands of the enemy, 'the regimental flag was stripped from the staff, torn in pieces, and its fragments divided among its defenders.*

*The national flag (presented by the loyal ladies of West Baltimore) was also secured from capture, and finally secreted in an adjoining field, where it was subsequently found by a portion of the First Vermont Cavalry, and returned to Colonel Kenly.* [3]

Three days later, as the Union prisoners of war were marched into the nearby town of Winchester, they found that at:

*. . . about 9 p.m., while passing through the main street a rebel band [that] was serenading "Stonewall" Jackson at the Taylor House. The General and his staff, with other officers and friends, were out on the portico of the hotel, the windows being crowded with ladies, gaily dressed, while the band was discoursing that favorite of Southern war tunes, "The Bonnie Blue Flag." No sooner did the prisoners hear the first strains of the band, than, with one accord, they all joined in singing the Star-Spangled Banner in a manner so spirited, and in tones so loud, as to entirely drown the music of the serenade. The effect produced upon the rebel guard by this outburst of patriotic feeling was such that they made little or no effort to suppress it, and the prisoners continued singing until they reached the quarters selected for them at the railroad depot.* [4]

The men of the 1st Maryland expected to be exchanged for Confederate prisoners within a few days (or weeks), but circumstances didn't allow for that.

The enlisted men were sent to Belle Island prison in Richmond, and the officers to a Prisoner of War camp in Salisbury, North Carolina.

Accompanying the officers to Salisbury was a four-legged turncoat, from the Confederate point of view. Shortly before the battle of Front Royal, "a young Mastiff of medium size and jetty blackness, except a white breast and a dash of white on each of his four paws," decided that his sympathies lay with the Union, and he

22

deserted his original master, "a rebel jailer in Front Royal, Virginia … in spite of all his master's efforts to detain him." [5]

*He proceeded with them to the battle-field—keeping company with the officers as he went along —and his first exploit was trying hard to unearth a cannon-ball which he had seen bury itself near him. Presently the shells began to scream and burst in the air all around him. When Jack saw them coming, instead of running to hide himself—as it is said many a blustering bully does—he ran barking after the fragments and trying to catch them; thinking, no doubt, that it was some pyrotechnic display got up for his especial amusement.[6]*

After the battle, the dog was dubbed "Union Jack" or just "Jack." Although it's doubtful that Jack's decision to join the Federals, and share their later confinement, was motivated by political convictions, it was made to seem that way by the author of a November 8, 1862, *Harper's Weekly* article, who met Jack shortly after he was paroled with others in his regiment.

*His manners are very gentle and even timid among his friends, but he is suspicious and fierce as a lion when among his enemies. Although born in Secessia, and breathing constantly the air of treason, he is intensely loyal to the Union, and betrays a hatred of any thing in the shape of a rebel, which many of our "conservative" and "neutral" loyalists in the North would do well to imitate.*

*This settled the question of Jack's bravery, and from this time forward he seemed to form an affection for our officers, and they for him, which nothing could alter, and he has accompanied them through all their vicissitudes and changes of prison to Richmond.*

*The stories told of this dog's sagacity and devotion would seem incredulous had they not come from the most varied and reliable sources. On the road, when our parched men were fainting from thirst, he would always run forward, and whenever he discovered a pool of water would rush back, barking loudly, to tell them of it. When they were supplied with only five crackers to each man for five days—with no meat—and our poor fellows were literally dying from starvation, this noble animal has been known to go and catch*

23

chickens for them and to bring them in his mouth! Or he would waylay every rebel horse or wagon passing with food, and bark imploringly for them to bring relief. On one occasion, when a sick and exhausted Union soldier had been left behind, Jack staid with him for several hours until a wagon took him up.

But one of the most remarkable features in his character is his utter hatred of the rebels. His actions, in this respect, really seemed to go beyond brute instinct. No kindness, no attempt at caressing could get the "gray-coats" to win him over or even induce him to take food from them; but he growled and snapped at them upon all occasions, until many threatened to shoot him. When they got to the Richmond prison, another large dog was there being fondled by a secesh officer, and Jack stood looking at both, apparently with the greatest hatred and disgust. When the officer left, the secesh dog tried to scrape an acquaintance with Jack, but the latter did not covet any such friendship. He rushed upon the canine rebel, gave him a sound thrashing, and, although larger than himself, fairly tossed him over his head.

Jack is a great disciplinarian. When on duty, he knows the various roll-calls so well that he pays no attention to any of them but one—that of his officers. As soon as he heard this, he used to run about in the greatest excitement, as if to call his friends together, and then, placing himself alongside of the drummer, would put up his nose and commence a long howl— the boys used to say answering to his name. In traveling he seemed to take the whole responsibility upon himself. Whenever the cars stopped he was invariably the first to jump off, and the whistle no sooner sounded than he was the first to jump on again.

But no character is perfect, and we are sorry to say there is a serious blemish in Jack's. He is an aristocrat of the first water; one of the regular out-and-out F. F. V.'s. From first to last—except to help them when in distress—he never would associate with privates, but always stuck fast to where the shoulder-straps were assembled. But, after all, in this respect poor Jack is only following the example of many a human toady and tuft-hunter that can be called to mind; and before we blame this young puppy for cringing to the rich and great, let us remember that he is not the only puppy who does so.

24

*Upon the whole, Jack is an immense favorite with all who know him, but especially the First Maryland regiment, who claim him as their own, and ... they expressed a determination of having, as soon as they got to Baltimore, a splendid collar made expressly for their favorite; and we shall be surprised if this lucky dog does not become a great lion in the monumental city.*[7]

The 1st Maryland returned to duty by early 1863 and participated in major campaigns throughout Virginia until the end of the war. We do not know whether Union Jack was still with them, or indeed, what became of him, since he's never mentioned again. We can only hope that he survived the terrible carnage, and was able to end his days in peace and comfort.

UNION JACK, THE PET OF OUR RICHMOND PRISONERS.

**This sketch of "Union Jack" appeared in the *Harper's Weekly*. Captured at Front Royal with 21 officers and 514 enlisted men of the 1st Maryland Infantry (U. S.), "Union Jack" and his comrades were held in Confederate prisons in 1862.** *(Harper's Weekly, November 8, 1862)*

**An unidentified man and his best friend taken in Sinclearville, New York.** *(Author's Collection)*

# Chapter 3

## The Littlest Mourner

After President Abraham Lincoln replaced the Army of Potomac's commanding general, George B. McClellan, with Major General Ambrose Everett Burnside, the latter tried to compensate for his predecessor's "timidity" by advancing on Fredericksburg, Virginia, in mid-November 1862, planning to assault Richmond. Arriving with vastly superior forces, (121,402 men supported by 312 pieces of artillery)[1] when just a few thousand Confederates occupied the town, Burnside encountered a spell of bad luck. The materials he needed to build pontoon bridges across the Rappahannock River were delayed for over a week. This gave the Confederates under General Robert E. Lee a chance to fortify the heights behind the town and bring in plenty of reinforcements.

By the time the Union built the pontoon bridges across the river and advanced its troops on December 11, the Confederates had 78,511 men supported by 275 guns,[2] most of which were well-entrenched on the high ground behind Fredericksburg. After occupying the town, where some Federals looted the abandoned houses, Burnside prepared a two-pronged attack for December 13.

The next two days witnessed a horrendous slaughter of Union men. By December 15, the Federals withdrew across the Rappahannock, after suffering 12,653 casualties.[3]

The 91st Pennsylvania Infantry, in its maiden battle, experienced its heaviest losses of the war during the first day of the engagement when it charged Marye's Heights. Confederate artillery blasted away at the Pennsylvanians from atop of the crest with murderous accuracy as the Keystoners made their charge. Nearly a quarter of the regiment's original 23 officers and 401 men present at the battle were lost making that futile charge.[4]

One of the Union casualties was a Philadelphia wheelwright named William H. Brown, who was 27 or 28 years old when he was struck down late in the afternoon, December 13, leaving behind him a widow Sarah, and four small children, all of whom were under the age of 8 at the time of his death.[5] One member of the family, however, had accompanied Sergeant Brown on his journey–a small dog whose name is lost to history. This dog remained loyal to his master unto death, and beyond.

*Saturday Evening Post* **27** December 1862 [Philadelphia]: FIDELITY OF A DOG ON THE BATTLE-FIELD – On the Monday after the contest, as Hon. John Covode [a member of Congress], in company with a number of officers, was passing over the battlefield beyond Fredericksburg, their attention was called to a small dog lying by a corpse. Mr. Covode halted a few minutes to see if life was extinct. Raising the coat from the man's face, he found him dead. The dog, looking wistfully up, ran to the dead man's face and kissed his silent lips. Such devotion in a small dog was so singular that Mr. Covode examined some papers upon the body, and found it to be that of Sergt. W. H. Brown, company C, 91st Pennsylvania.

The dog was shivering with the cold, but refused to leave his master's body, and as the coat was thrown over his face again he seemed very uneasy, and tried to get under it to the man's face. He had, it seems, followed the regiment into battle, and stuck to his master, and when he fell remained with him, refusing to leave him or to eat anything. As the party returned, an ambulance was carrying the corpse to a little grove of trees for interment, and the little dog following, the only mourner at that funeral, as the hero's comrades had been called to some other point.[6]

No one knows what later happened to this small canine mourner after Brown was buried.

**Civil War CDV of soldier with dog. Soldier stands next to a table while his faithful canine companion is perched atop a trunk. Inscription on the back reads Robt. Sharp.** *(Author's Collection)*

**"Fox", mascot of the 143<sup>rd</sup> New York Infantry.**
*(U. S. Army Military History Institute. rg98s)*

# Chapter 4

## Curly and the 11<sup>th</sup> Ohio Infantry

In April 1861, members of what became the 11th Ohio Volunteer Infantry offered their services as artillerymen to the governor of Ohio. Although Governor William Dennison, Jr., like his counterparts in other states still loyal to the Union, was recruiting volunteers to fulfill Lincoln's initial request for 75,000 troops, he apparently had less interest in artillerymen than infantry regiments, so the unit switched to mustering in as infantrymen.[1] The smallest recruit joining the 11th Ohio was a liver-colored water spaniel with a few white spots, which the soldiers adopted as their pet, naming him Curly.

While in Camp Dennison, Ohio, on April 19, 1861, Mrs. Shellabarger, who said she had too many dogs, gave Curly to Private John H. Crouse of Company A, who brought the puppy to his comrades as a new recruit. Crouse told his fellow soldiers that Mrs. Shellabarger thought the dog was "no good on earth for anything she knew of, so he ought to make a good soldier."[2] It seems Mrs. Shellabarger had low regard for both the puppy and for soldiering. Fortunately, Curly's intelligence and bravery under fire soon belied his original owner's harsh words.

> *Curly was a remarkable animal. If he was not in possession of reasoning faculties, his instincts approached so nearly to that human gift as to make a distinction unnecessary. He was as well acquainted with the members of the Regiment as any one, and if he could not call their names he was never mistaken in identifying an Eleventh man. He knew as well when a march or movement was in contemplation as if he understood every word of the order issued, and made his preparations accordingly. It was his custom upon receiving his "rations" to consume as much as he required, and then bury the balance. If, before he became hungry again, he noticed preparations for anything unusual going on in camp, he would immediately resurrect and eat his "reserves" and then patiently wait to take his place in the column.[3]*

Thanks to his intelligence and good looks–described by 1st Lieutenant Thomas L. Steward as having "beautiful brown eyes, wide, intelligent forehead, with a white face–Curly won the hearts of

31

all in his regiment. Unfortunately, not every soldier was as fond of canine mascots as the ordinary men of the 11$^{th}$ Ohio.

On August 17, 1862, while the regiment was being ferried along the Kanawha River toward the Ohio, a certain major (or "majah" as he was derisively called by one man) decided that the various dogs attached to the companies were becoming a burden. Therefore, he ordered an unlucky soldier to "unload the mongrel brood" that night. The major had a man detailed to "throw every cur overboard and let him swim for his life, either to free Ohio or the 'sacred isle'" (presumably heaven).

When the man assigned to this loathsome task approached the 11$^{th}$ Ohio's Company A with his orders, however, he was apparently told in no uncertain terms that if he threw Curly overboard, he would be a "goner." The man reported this to the major, and the order to dump dogs into the river was revoked, saving Curly from drowning or, at minimum, a long swim and separation from his friends.[4]

Unfortunately, this incident didn't mark the last time that Curly barely escaped death. Although the dog stuck to his command at battles such as South Mountain, where the regiment fought the enemy hand-to-hand, and Antietam, where their Colonel Augustus H. Coleman fell mortally wounded leading the attack on Burnside's Bridge, Curly was nearly killed on October 28, 1862, by one of his own friends after the regiment was moved west to Summerville, West Virginia.

> *I was target practicing a little, when Curly ran into the bushes behind the target. Captain Staley fired about that time, and caught Curly in the neck, just about where he wore his badge, which bore this legend:*
>
> *"I am company A's dog. Whose dog are you?"*
>
> *Captain Hatfield detailed a nurse, and Curly was placed in a wagon, carefully nursed, and soon reported for duty. He got into a goodly number of scrapes for a member of such a modest, moral regiment as the Eleventh Ohio was reputed to be.*[5]

Curly's finest hour occurred at the battle of Chickamauga in late September of 1863. By that time, the 11$^{th}$ Ohio was part of Major General William S. Rosecrans' Army of the Cumberland, which had just driven the Confederates out of Chattanooga, Tennessee, an army commanded by General Braxton Bragg, for whom Fort Bragg, North Carolina, was later named. Bragg was determined to retake

Chattanooga, and soon had a plan to defeat part of Rosecrans' army, and then move back into the city.

Late in the morning, September 20, as Bragg's men were pounding at Rosecrans' left flank, Rosecrans was told that a gap had opened in his line. In order to plug this gap, which turned out to be fictitious, Rosecrans opened a *real* gap, and the charging rebels commanded by General James Longstreet immediately took advantage of the mistake, driving one-third of the Union army, including Rosecrans himself, from the field. Major General George H. Thomas took command of the Union forces, and managed to repulse determined Confederate assaults until night fell. After this, the Union withdrew back to Chattanooga, leaving the Confederates in charge of the surrounding heights.

The 11th Ohio succeeded in fighting off multiple Confederate attacks that day, until they were finally ordered to withdraw as part of the retreat to Chattanooga. Curly did not join the retreat, however, preferring to tend to his wounded comrades. Lieutenant Thomas Steward described Curly's actions at the battle:

*At Chickamauga, Curly elected to stay on the field to take care of our wounded, as he knew how it was himself. Think of the friendly, pitying glance of their mute comrade as he passed from one wounded sufferer to another and could render no aid; but he was true and resisted the blandishments of the confederate who tempted him with a morsel of food to leave his old comrades. When General Thomas arranged for the parole and return of our wounded, Curly took advantage of the flag of truce, and came in with the unfortunates.*[6]

Of Curly, Lieutenant Joshua H. Horton wrote:

*On the march, he was always in advance, and in a fight was ever busy on the skirmish line. He was in his element when brisk firing was going on, and was never so happy as when in a "scrimmage." He took a prominent part in all the battles in which the Regiment was engaged, but particularly distinguished himself at Chickamauga, where he was taken prisoner. He refused to leave the field when our forces retired, but remained with the wounded, manifesting his sympathy for their misfortunes in an unmistakable manner. After the battle, the wounded were removed under flag of truce, at which time Curly made his escape and "joined his Company."*

*He was soon after missed from his quarters, and for several days nothing could be heard of him. It was reported after a while that a Captain in an Illinois regiment had a dog, answering to Curly's description, confined in his tent. Several of Company A boys, headed by Jules Ogier, called on the Captain who denied having the dog. Looking about the premises, the boys saw Curly fastened by a chain in an enclosure in the rear of the tent, but the Captain protested that it was not the dog for which they were searching. Curly, hearing the boys, gave such evidence of acquaintance that several officers in the tent spoke in favor of the boys' right to him, and the Captain was obliged peaceably to give him up. (It is perhaps not necessary to say that the boys would not have considered "shoulder straps" of any consequence had not their claims to their dog been promptly recognized. And if it had been necessary, they would have had "backing" in every member of the Eleventh).*[7]

Two companies of the regiment accompanied General William Tecumseh Sherman on his famous "march to the sea," but most of the men, and Curly, were mustered out after a three year enlistment in late June of 1864 at Camp Dennison, Ohio.

Curly nearly did not make it. He was accidentally shoved off the moving train, but was soon recovered. Whether Curley fell or was pushed, all the sources agree that he broke his leg in the fall.

*Upon the regiment's return home in 1864, Curly was crowded off the car at Bowling Green, Ky., breaking a fore leg in falling. Before he could be recovered the train proceeded, and he was given up for lost. However, one of our stragglers found him, fixed up his leg, and forwarded him to Louisville. From there he was sent to Osborne, Ohio, where he remained for a time in the care of Comrade Baggott [John, Oliver or Watson]. The boys in Dayton desiring to have him there, he was accordingly sent to the writer [Lieutenant Thomas Steward], who gave him a home.*[8]

Curly lived the remainder of his life in peace, a veteran of many battles. Like many veterans, he even attended regimental reunions after the war.

**"Curly" of the 11th Ohio Infantry always wore a badge around his neck with the inscription, "I am Company's A's Dog, Whose Dog are You?"** *(11th Inf. Regt. Proceedings of the . . . . Annual Reunion of the Eleventh Ohio Infantry)*

At the second annual reunion of the 11th Ohio, held in Dayton, Ohio, on September 20, 1870, exactly five years after the final day at Chickamauga, Curly received thunderous applause and shouts from his former comrades when he took the stage.

> *At this juncture 'Curly,' the old Regimental dog, was introduced on the stage, and as soon as beheld was received with shouts of applause. 'Curly' has quite a history, which if properly written would fill a volume. Before starting from camp Dennison into the three years service 'Curly' was secured and at once mustered in as a member in good standing, and through the long and arduous campaign and many bloody battles, well and faithfully did he perform his duties. At the terrible battle of Chickamauga he was taken prisoner, and remained for two days at the hospital, within the enemy's lines. . . . 'Curly' may well be considered a veteran dog, and is justly entitled to spend the remainder of his days in rest and peace.* [9]

By the time of the second annual reunion of the regiment, Curly was becoming lame, rheumatic and mangy, refusing to sleep anywhere but in the house with his old comrade. At night, he would howl from the pain of his wound and his broken leg caused him to limp badly. At this point, his owner sent him to the Central Branch,

National Home for Disabled Volunteer Soldiers in Dayton, where he was admitted as a hero by his fellow veterans, who gave him a warm bunk in the engine house.[10] While living among disabled veterans, Curly, by his instinctive care and companionship, could be considered one of the nation's first unofficial pet therapists.

> The Eleventh boys wanted Curly at all reunions, so a comrade in Dayton, took him. Later he was sent to the central branch of the national soldiers' home, D.V.S. at Dayton. He fared sumptuously there and lived to the good old age of twelve years, when he died amongst his soldier friends and was buried by them in the hallowed and patriotic precincts of that beautiful place.[11]

His headboard was inscribed with the challenge that he wore on his collar during life: "I am Curly, Company A's dog, whose dog are you?"[12]

He was almost certainly buried at the Central Branch Home for D. V. S. in Dayton, still an active Veterans Administration hospital, whose cemetery is now the Dayton National Cemetery. According to sources at the American Veterans Heritage Center in Dayton, Curly's marker was wooden, and has since been lost to time. Wooden head boards began to be replaced by stone markers in 1874, but Curly was interred just before then, making a search for Curley's headstone and finale resting place futile.[13]

# Chapter 5

## Kidnapped, Captured, or Lost

After a hard day's work, and whenever "the blues" come, dogs can be a morale booster and a source of comfort, especially during times of war. For men separated from friends and loved ones, subject to endless weeks of boredom, punctuated by moments of terror, canine mascots have been highly prized as pets and companions. Unfortunately, some Civil War dogs were so prized that they were sought after by soldiers who had the audacity to kidnap or capture them from their original units. One of the most famous dognapping victims was named Stonewall Jackson

During the fierce fighting around Richmond, Virginia, during the summer of 1862, an artillerist of the Richmond Howitzers, 1st Company, noticed a little puppy. Robert Stiles, who enlisted as a 1st Lieutenant with Howitzers, documented this:

*The Howitzer dog, whom we christened "Stonewall Jackson," came to us a mere puppy in the summer of 1862, after the battles around Richmond, and while we were waiting for the re-equipment of the battery. He was a Welsh fice, very small, but beautifully formed, gleaming white in color, with a few spots of jet black, his hair fine and short, and lying close and smooth. He did not carry guns enough, metaphorically speaking, to amount to much in a canine encounter, but he was a born warrior, a perfect hero in battle. When our guns were in action he was always careering wildly about them, and in any pause of their hoarse thunders the shrill treble of his tiny bark was always to be heard.*

*He was an intelligent, companionable little chap, and the boys taught him some uncommon tricks. His special master, teacher, patron and friend was clearly old "Van," [Sergeant John Van Lew McCreery, 1st Company]—chief of the second detachment—who could do anything from shoeing a horse to making a clock out of pine bark, and must of necessity be always doing something, even if it were but training a puppy. Van taught Stonewall to attend roll-call, and to sit up on his haunches, next to him, on the advanced rank of non-commissioned officers, and he made a little pipe for him, which Stonewall would hold firmly in his mouth when Van had once inserted it between his teeth. Then when the orderly sergeant, before beginning the roll, called "Pipes out!" Van would stoop and slip Stonewall's pipe from his mouth to his left paw, which would then instantly drop to his side with the other, and the little corporal would stand, or sit, stiffly and staunchly in the position of a soldier, eyes front, until the company was dismissed.* [1]

The men of the Richmond Howitzers were very protective of Stonewall, according to Robert Stiles, a northerner who spent his formative years in the Old Dominion, prompting him to enlist with the Confederate army after the battle of First Manassas July 21, 1861. (The Richmond Howitzers was largely composed of well-educated young men, and Stiles was a graduate of Yale and Columbia universities.) The soldiers were not about to entrust Stonewall's life to Providence, though the dog's namesake (General Thomas J. "Stonewall" Jackson) probably would have.

*It was surprising that he was not lost or killed in action, especially when we had to change our position rapidly under fire, which was very often. Under such circumstances, whoever happened to be nearest the little fellow, if by a frantic dive he could manage to get him in time, would lift the lid of a limber chest, drop him in an empty partition, and clap the lid down again before the gun dashed off with the rest; but as soon as it came into battery in the new position, No. 6, before getting at his fuses, would first lift the little warrior from his dark, close quarters and drop him on the ground, where, in a twinkling, he would recover his balance, resume his part in the fight and keep it up until, in another move, he was again imprisoned in transitu, either in an ammunition chest or under someone's arm.* [2]

As Stonewall gained a reputation for courage and cleverness, envy spread among other units serving in the Army of Northern Virginia, making Stonewall the target of kidnapping conspiracies. On one occasion, Stonewall disappeared from the unit, and was later discovered in the camp of Brigadier General Harry Hays' Louisiana Creoles, "tied to a tent pole with the men gathered around, feeding and petting him."

When members of the Richmond Howitzers confronted the thieves, the ensuing argument nearly turned into a deadly "friendly-fire" incident. The Louisianans claimed the dog was a hungry stray that had wondered into camp. Just as tempers reached the boiling point, Stonewall Jackson tried to break free and run toward the artillerymen. The Creoles conceded and reluctantly returned the dog to its owners, [3] but Robert Stiles recalls it was not for long:

> *Stonewall was stolen from us several times by Harry Hayes' brigade, his Louisiana Creoles having the ungovernable passion of the French soldier for pets. At last the cunning thieves succeeded in hiding him, and we lost him finally, to the deep regret, not to say grief, of every man in the battery.* [4]

* * *

Not all soldiers were as respectful of canines as the Richmond Howitzers or Louisiana Creoles.

One afternoon, two members of the Richmond Howitzers, J. B. Lambert and 17-year-old Carlton McCarthy (mayor of Richmond 1904-1908), decided to take a detour from the main road during one of the company's marches in search of a home-cooked meal. Soon, they came upon a Virginia farmhouse owned by Sir Ronald Gatewood, who demonstrated a strange lack of Southern hospitality.

> *[He] was cold-mannered, the hardest man to thaw out I ever met. We tried every plan on him; still he remained brusque, unapproachable, and even peevish. We could get no satisfaction from him, and almost despaired of accomplishing anything. Finally, we said: 'Sir Ronald, where is your spring?' He pointed to the locality, and we asked if he would at least lend us a bucket, which he brought. We remarked: 'You need water in cooking, of course.' So we brought him three or four buckets full of that indispensable fluid. This moved him. Indeed, it was the magic 'open sesame' to his heart, it was the touchstone. He then said: 'I will see if the old lady will get you a good dinner,' and it was just for that most desirable point we were maneuvering.*
>
> *In a short time dinner was announced and we enjoyed a good square meal. In the course of conversation, we found out why Sir Ronald was so hard to influence at first. It appears that a few days previous, a party of infantrymen had called upon him, and while the meal was being prepared for them, they got a pair of scissors and trimmed his dog up resembling*

39

*a lion in appearance, that is, they cut all the hair off the body except his shoulders. It was a handsome shepherd dog, and valued very highly by its owner. Of course, we told Sir Ronald we sympathized with him, and pronounced the act a piece of vandalism and were not surprised at his being enraged at soldiers. Before parting we made a firm friend of the gentleman.* [5]

\* \* \*

Another dog captured from its regiment was Candy. The little white Fox Terrier dog was so named because he had been given to Isaac Stein of the 4th Texas Infantry, Company B, by an old Austin, Texas, candy maker named Montana. [6]

The 4th Texas was one of three Texas regiments of the famed Texas Brigade, part of Robert E. Lee's Army of Northern Virginia. General John Bell Hood excelled early in the war as their brigade and division leader. The regiment tasted combat on the Virginia Peninsula on May 7, 1862, at Eltham's Landing, but its first major engagement took place on June 27 at the battle of Gaines' Mill. Here, the 4th Texas established a reputation for fierce fighting by helping to break the Union line on Turkey Hill. [7]

During the battle, however, the 4th Texas nearly lost Candy. In the confusion, he became separated from the regiment, and wasn't seen until the following morning. Val C. Giles, who later wrote about his years with the 4th Texas in *Rags and Hope*, described what happened:

> *. . . [N]ext morning when the burying detail was sent out from the regiment they found "Candy" cuddled up under the arm of poor John Summers (of Company B), who was killed the evening before. There was not a man in the regiment who would not have divided the last piece of "hardtack" he had with "Candy" He never swam a river or waded through the mud unless he wanted to. There was always some soldier ready to pick him up and carry him.* [8]

Despite the sentiments of the men who cared for him, Candy became a casualty at Sharpsburg (also Antietam). He was captured on the bloodiest day in American history, a day when the 4th Texas suffered its greatest losses of any single battle of the war, losing 57 killed, 130 wounded and 23 captured. [9] No doubt, Candy was not included in the official report of the 23 captured.

The battle of Sharpsburg was the first of two attempts by Robert E. Lee to carry the war to the North. After his great victory at Second Manassas in August 1862, Lee marched his army into Maryland, hoping to gain an advantage in the war.

On September 17, at about 5:30 a. m., the battle began as forces commanded by Union General Joseph Hooker advanced on both sides of the Hagerstown Turnpike toward a white-walled Dunkard Church, which the Federals thought was a schoolhouse, since it had no steeple. (The Dunkards believed steeples were immodest).

Just before 7:00 a. m., General Hood was told that his division was desperately needed to stave off Federal attacks that were stretching the Confederate army's left flank, under Stonewall Jackson, to the breaking point. Hood's men had just received a visit from the commissary wagon, providing them with rations of salt pork, beef and flour around daybreak. As they began cooking their first hot meal in days, Union artillery started firing into their position. The interruption of their breakfast, combined with the sudden order to advance and support Jackson, infuriated the hungry soldiers.

Forming up in a line west of the Dunkard Church, the division marched toward the sounds of battle, and soon encountered fierce Federal resistance. Despite this, the Texans pushed the Federals back into Miller's Cornfield. Following the retreating foe, the Confederates advanced to the base of a small plateau, about 300 yards from their starting position. The men of the 4th Texas, however, soon found themselves unable to return fire or even see the enemy, thanks to other Confederate troops in their front and the dense battle smoke. They were ordered to lie down, but almost as soon as the order was given, General Hood had them moved to support the left-most regiments of the Texas Brigade.

The 4th Texas charged near a fence on the eastern side of the Hagerstown Turnpike, where it faced three Union regiments as well as artillery fire from a battery. It's little wonder that the 4th Texas sustained such horrific casualties. During the fight in the cornfield, Candy was captured by the Federals. A wounded corporal of the 4th Texas, George L. Robertson, while lying in a Federal field hospital, saw Candy being triumphantly paraded around the Federal camp as the littlest prisoner captured during the battle. Engraved on his collar was "Candy, Co. B, 4th Texas Reg't." Candy was never seen or heard from again by the Texans. [10]

Although Candy was captured by the enemy, it's doubtful that the men of the 4th Texas were any more heartbroken than the men of the Richmond Howitzers, who had lost their dog to "friends."

Candy was luckier than many of the soldiers who met on the battlefield that day. Federal losses were 12,401; Confederate losses were 10,318.[11] Neither side achieved a decisive victory, but Lee's failure to successfully invade the Union allowed President Lincoln to claim the victory he needed to issue the Emancipation Proclamation on January 1, 1863.

One member of the 4th Texas, at least, was later reunited with a beloved dog. After the surrender at Appomattox, Val C. Giles returned to his home near Austin, Texas, on a Sunday evening in September 1865. He'd been away for nearly four and a half years.

*Father and mother were not expecting me and were not home, but my dog, Brave, was on guard. When I left home to join the Army in 1861, he was about three years old.*

*It was not a 'deep-mouthed welcome' that greeted me as I drew near, but a gruff emphatic warning to keep out. Old Brave, now a veteran of more than eight years, took me for a tramp, and was not very far from right about it.*

*I began to talk to him; he quit barking, sat down and listened.*

*'Brave, old boy,' I said,' don't you know me?'*

*He cocked up one ear and looked at me sideways.*

*It finally dawned on him who I was, and he came toward me wagging his tail. I opened the gate and he landed on my breast with both paws. I petted him on the head for a moment, then he broke away and circled wildly all around me, expressing in his dumb way his delight at my return.[12]*

**"A little pup brought from the South during the Civil War, Frankie Burnett."** *(Author's Collection)*

Battery A of the 1<sup>st</sup> Illinois Light Artillery Volunteers was assembled in Chicago, made its first appearance in April 1861, and participated in many of the most famous battles of the Civil War, including Forts Donelson and Henry, Shiloh, the siege at Vicksburg, Kennesaw Mountain, and Atlanta. From the standpoint of mascots, there are two notable, even peculiar, aspects to the tale of the 1<sup>st</sup> Illinois, as told by Charles B. Kimball.

Kimball makes mention of the fact that not just dogs, but a wide variety of other creatures often served as mascots. "Any live thing, biped or quadruped, from a chicken to a pig, or a little contraband coon" might be found traveling with the men on their long marches.

*A Wisconsin regiment had an American eagle, "Old Abe," which sat proudly perched upon a frame over their banner while being carried on all their marches and through all their engagements. A company in the 51<sup>st</sup> Illinois Infantry had a kitten.*

*. . . one of our boys even entered the reptile kingdom to obtain one of these necessary articles. J. F. Stackhouse a natural scientist and naturalist, (surnamed "Snakehouse" for obvious reasons) captured a large yellow moccasin which he tamed and petted as ordinary human beings would a kitten. He devoted all his spare time to gathering snakes, lizards, toads, bugs, etc., and his collection was a source of mortal terror to all his messmates, who feared they would escape and become partners in their bunks and blankets.*[13]

Kimball is rather casual in mentioning that, before reaching Larkinsville, Alabama, in January 1864, "we had the misfortune to lose our 'mascot,' which had been constantly with us since we left Paducah," about 18 months earlier.

*[Tony,] Battery "A's" mascot was a, "thorough-bred" mongrel dog, a cross between a Scotch terrier and something else unknown; but he was a dog among a thousand all the same. He came to us in Paducah from some infantry regiment. He seemed to consider an artillery man a superior being, and looked with perfect disdain on*

**Civil War era carte de visite showing a man with a large puppy dog.** *(Author's Collection)*

*any infantryman that tried to make any advances toward an acquaintance. Among his many traits he considered it his sacred duty to always carry something when on a march. Any old shoe, bootleg, bone or stick that he could pick up in the morning, would be carried all day with unfailing regularity. Charley Smith, in writing to a brother, in 1862, who was a minister in Franklinville, Ill., told the story of our "mascot," which is worthy of reproduction here:*

*"Our Battery dog is barking at some loose horse. That reminds me of my carelessness in not before describing so illustrious a character as that dog. He is the pet of the Battery, known as well to the horses as the men and has been associated with our interests over eighteen months. He owns no one as master, but all. On the march he will follow no one gun, but persists in leading or going beside the advance piece. He has been in four battles and twice wounded, once at Donelson and once at Shiloh. At this latter fight he learned caution, and now at the sound of firing, he will hunt a tree with as much zeal as his biped friends. What is the most singular is his diet. In this respect, he is a thorough old soldier. While in camp, fresh meat, bread and potatoes, too, if we have them, are not too good for him. On the march he takes his 'hard tack' and bacon, and not a man but will give him a share. If we are on short rations he takes a meal of corn or oats with some horse. He has had as many names as the 'Old Man of the Sea,' his last has stuck to him longest, 'Tony.' In personal appearance he is not calculated to impress one with a sense of his faculties; but shaggy, black mongrel as he is, he knows more than some men, and fears no dog that lives. Although often worsted in encounters with superior-sized dogs, he never leaves the field in disgrace, but his tail is just as high over his back as ever, and one could not help thinking that the old fellow feels conscious that he has done his duty. Rights, he is invaluable at the grain pile, in driving away stray horses, and has often been my companion in standing guard. He is never absent from 'roll call,' however far he may be away, chasing a horse or otherwise, the sound of the 'assembly' has just as potent an influence on him as on us. He never loses us, and never takes any other battery for us. In fact, he is a 'wonderful dorg,' and the Boys think the world of him."*[14]

Perhaps Charles E. Smith, who joined the unit as an 18-year-old student from Northwestern University, was much more attached to Tony than Kimball, or at least more sentimental. Or Perhaps Kimball was so heartbroken by the loss of Battery A's pet, that he couldn't bring himself to say more than what Smith had already written so well in his letter home. Either way, Tony's fate has been lost to history, just as he was lost.

We'll never know whether he was mortally wounded or decided that he'd had enough of army life, and then wandered to the nearest farmhouse where the owners accepted him as a member of their non-military family.

**Alfred R. Waud made this sketch of the Army of the Potomac's movement near Falmouth, Virginia, on January 21, 1863, entitled "Winter Campaigning." The sketch was published in the Harper's Weekly, February 14, 1863, edition. Inclement weather and excessive mud brought a halt to the movement and the army returned to winter quarters. Waud included a dog in the sketch following behind a soldier on the lower left-hand portion of the sketch.** *(Courtesy of the Library of Congress)*

**A dog and a drummer boy. stamped on the back: "Photographed by J. B. Mathias, New Philadelphia, Ohio."** *(Author's Collection)*

# Chapter 6

## Eternal Guardian

Washington G. Pollock was born in Dutchess County, New York[1] and joined the 20th New York State Militia, Ulster Guard, in the fall of 1861. Shortly after, the 20th New York State Militia was redesignated as the 80th New York State Volunteers. This unfortunate Union private and his dog were killed a year later at the battle of Antietam. The dog's name is not known, but he or she was killed that same day, trying to protect the body of Private Pollock. His canine companion in life became his companion in death.

It is not known how or when the bond between this man and dog was forged. One source gives us a clue as to how long the bond was formed but the time seems too short for such a bond, except that the dog was a Newfoundlander with a big heart. Perhaps the black Newfoundlander was the personal pet of Private Pollock and accompanied him from the verdant Catskill Mountains near the Hudson River to his destruction by a Maryland creek. Perhaps the dog joined the 80th New York sometime after Pollock was mustered into service in September and October of 1861. Or maybe the dog was a Washingtonian that had fled the muddy city while Pollock was performing picket duty along the Potomac in the spring of 1862.

We may never know the details. But this much we do know: This faithful friend followed his master to the grave, because the dog dared guard the man's corpse in a blood-soaked cornfield. Here then, is an account of what happened.

*So often during the morning in this hotly contested part of the field the Union troops were to drive the enemy back until it seemed they would break his lines, only to have reinforcements brought in against them and be forced back in turn with heavy losses. Lee was taking troops from all other parts of the field and using his reserves to stop the Union advance.*

*The 80th was soon to feel the effect of this policy. More men were brought up against it and Hardenbergh [colonel of the 80th New York Infantry] was forced to fall back. This was done with deliberation, the Ulster men firing as rapidly as they could load while the battery and right wing hammered the oncoming Confederates.*

*Hardenbergh's men rejoined their comrades defending the guns, which were belching forth an iron hail into the enemy advance.*

*The men in grey continued their forward movement despite the terrible fire until they reached the guns and drove the gunners from their pieces. They held them but momentarily; the concentrated fire of the Ulster boys at close range was more than they could stand. They fell back to the cover of a small ridge in their rear. Gunners and their supporters exulted, but not for long.*

*Reorganized and supported by additional troops, the Confederates again plunged forward. Greeted by heavy federal fire, they responded to it as they advanced over open fields in a manner that won the admiration of the defenders. Capt. Campbell double-shotted his guns with canister, holding his fire until the intrepid foe got within fifty feet of him. When the ninety-four iron balls from each gun were discharged in their faces the attacking column almost ceased to be. The havoc was frightful and when the men of the 80th sprang forward to charge them with the bayonet it was more than human endurance could stand. The remaining men of the gallant column fell back to their lines and the guns were not again assaulted.*

*This was the end of the battle so far as the Ulster Guard was concerned. So it was for most of the regiments of the First Corps. They had won limited objectives, had driven a wedge into Jackson's line that for a moment seemed fatal to it. When the ever-aggressive Hood came up and delivered one of his fierce countercharges the Union advance was overwhelmed and driven back. Hooker was wounded and carried from the field. On his way to the rear he noted that the cornfield had been cut down as though the owner, Miller, had considered it was harvest time. Hooker's artillery had sprayed it so effectively with shot and shell it would never need the cornknife. In between the tall stalks there were hundreds of dead and dying Confederates who had sought concealment while firing upon the advancing federals.*

*While remaining in position and under fire to a limited extent, the Ulster Guard suffered no more losses at Antietam. According to Col. Gates it had but 135 officers and men in line of battle. Its percentage of loss, by his figures, was 35 per cent. Ten men and one officer were killed in action.*

*Thirty-eight men and two officers were wounded. Seven of the wounded men died and three men were missing. Among the dead was W. J. Pollock of Company H. Over his body when found, was that of a beautiful black Newfoundland dog which had joined the company on its march from Fredericksburg. Fed and cared for by the men, the animal followed them into battle at South Mountain where it seemed indifferent to minie balls whistling around it as well as the fire of artillery and the rattle of musketry. Faithful to the man it considered its new master, the dog evidently tried to protect his body when Pollock fell— only to lose its own life.[2]*

Reporting this incident an article in the *Baltimore American,* September 23, 1862, said in part:

*Passing back again through the woods two Rebel colonels and one brigadier were found on the ground, and interspersed with the multitudes of their fallen were so many of those in the National uniform that at a glance one might see how fearful was the cost of the victory. Upon one dead body was found a large black dog, dead also from some chance shot which had struck him while stretched upon his master's corpse caressingly, his fore-paws across the man's breast. Ride where one might for a space of a mile and a half in width in places, and four or five miles in length, the dead were on every side, interspersed with the arms that had fallen from their hands.[3]*

A touching story—but it may not be entirely accurate. Because the study of history is sometimes not exact, it comes as no surprise that this heroic dog may *not* have belonged to Private Pollack at all. In fact, some believe the black Newfoundlander was the personal pet of Captain Werner Von Bachelle, who commanded Company F of the 6th Wisconsin Volunteer Infantry which belong to the famed Iron Brigade.

Like the 80th New York Infantry, the 6th Wisconsin Infantry faced the same murderous fire in the same Antietam cornfield on the same day in September 1862.

An ex-officer of the French army trained in the Napoleonic school of warfare, Bachelle was too young to have fought with Napoleon Bonaparte, but it's said that he also "was imbued with the doctrine of fatalism" and well-loved by his men.[4] Rufus R. Dawes was appointed major of the 6<sup>th</sup> Wisconsin Infantry in 1862, lieutenant colonel in 1863, and colonel in 1864 kept a journal through the war and after the war he combined it with his campaign letters to write *Service with the Sixth Wisconsin Volunteers*. Published in 1890 Dawes recorded this:

> *Bachelle had a fine Newfoundland dog, which had been trained to perform military salutes and many other remarkable things. In camp, on the march, and in the line of battle, this dog was his constant companion. The dog was by his side when he fell. Our line of men left the body when they retreated, but the dog stayed with his dead master, and was found on the morning of the 19<sup>th</sup> of September lying dead upon his body. We buried him with his master. So far as we knew, no family or friends mourned for poor Bachelle, and it is probable that he was joined in death by his most devoted friend on earth.* [5]

Man and dog rested in this grave for five years until Bachelle was reburied beneath headstone #858 in Antietam National Cemetery in Sharpsburg, Maryland. No one knows whether the bones of the Newfoundlander were also moved to this final resting place. [6] No one knows whether there were *two* black Newfoundlanders killed on that day while guarding the corpses of two slain masters, or whether one of the stories is untrue.

# Chapter 7

## Tinker Runs the Union Blockade

Despite invaluable contributions to their respective nations, many men and mascots, North and South, received little glory, or even credit, for their dash and daunting accomplishments. Foremost among the unsung heroes of the sunny South were the sailors who dared to run the Union naval blockade, which stretched from Virginia into the Gulf of Mexico and up the Mississippi River to Illinois. Most blockade runners picked up their contraband from Nassau, Bahamas, and from Bermuda to deliver to Confederate entry ports in Wilmington, North Carolina, and Charleston, South Carolina, along the Atlantic coast.

All kinds of sailing vessels, more than 300 of them, made up the U. S. blockade squadron on the Atlantic Coast, including three-deckers, monitors, ironclads, and side-wheels. To outrun the Union blockade ships, Confederate blockade runners were light weight, with a shallow draft.[1]

Although most blockade ships were painted gray to blend with the nighttime horizon, boilers belching black smoke announced their position. Some had hinged masts so they could be lowered out of sight, while others had their masts removed. Some ships were fitted with telescopic funnels to better identify the enemy from afar. The lack of lighthouses made deliveries even more dangerous, since they sailed under the cover of night.[2] Captain Michael P. Usina, a former riverboat pilot on the Savannah River, was among the Confederate blockade runners, whom he characterized this way in an 1893 speech to members of The Confederate Veterans Association:

> *The men who ran the blockade had to be men who could stand fire without returning it. It was a business in which every man took his life in his hands, and he so understood it. An ordinarily brave man had no business on a blockade runner. He who made a success of it was obliged to have the cunning of a fox, the patience of a Job, and the bravery of a Spartan warrior. Uncle Sam wanted at first to treat them as pirates and was never satisfied to consider them contrabandists. The runners must not be armed and must not resist, they must simply be cool and*

*quick and watchful, and for the rest trust to God and their*
*good ship to deliver them safely to their friends.[3]*

Many Americans believe that the early phases of the Civil War witnessed an unbroken string of brilliant Confederate victories at famous battles such as Manassas, Fredericksburg, and Chancellorsville. But when considering the various, sometimes mundane, puzzle pieces that had to be assembled to achieve victory, the Union may have been on its way to success by early 1862, thanks to its own unsung heroes, the seamen who enforced the blockade of Southern ports with their small armada of ships.

Usina was a Menorcan, descended from the inhabitants of Manorca, a large island in the Mediterranean Sea, off the coast of France and Spain. They had settled in Saint Augustine, Florida. Although he was of European stock, Usina was wholly devoted to the Confederacy. He enlisted in 1861 in Company A, 8th Georgia Infantry Regiment, also known as Oglethorp's Rifles, and participated in the battle of First Manassas. During the fight, however, he was severely wounded in the leg and eventually was sent home to recover.[4]

Not long afterward, as the Confederate navy was being organized, Usina was made captain of his own blockade runner, which he used to ferry supplies to American ports such as Wilmington and Savannah from Bermuda and the Bahamas. He was a proud and daring member of the Confederate Navy, and on more than one occasion he narrowly escaped capture. In one instance, he was boarded by a Union naval officer, who seemed to know a great deal about Usina and his crew. The Confederate captain denied his identity until the Union officer produced a photograph of Usina with vital bits of information written on the back. It seems that some photographers at Nassau in the Bahamas were making money by selling pictures of Confederate blockade runners to the enemy.[5]

Usina reluctantly attributed some of these narrow escapes to a good luck charm. This charm was not a rabbit's foot, but a living, four-legged Terrier named Tinker.

*. . . I do not think I am given to superstition, yet I had*
*with me a mascot who, I believe, was at that time one of*
*the most widely known dogs that ever existed. I was known*
*as the man that owned the dog! He was photographed at*
*Bermuda, and the artist realized quite a neat sum from the*
*sale of his pictures. He was left with me by a shipmate who*

*died at sea, and when dying frequently called for 'Tinker.' I cherished him for his master's sake, and afterwards became warmly attached to him for his own. He was a terrier, a great ratter, and fond of the water. He was my constant companion. He seemed to know when we were approaching the enemy, and to be on the alert, and when under fire would follow me step for step.*

*It was our custom, in the event of capture or destruction of the ship, to prepare the boats for leaving the ship the afternoon before running through the fleet. He seemed to inspect the work and devote most particular attention to the Captain's boat, and the sailors wondered how he knew one boat from another, but he certainly did.*

*When I placed my chief officer, Nelson, in command of the 'Armstrong,' I induced some of my men, whom I knew could be depended upon, to go with him, as I was more than anxious to have him succeed. Among those that I approached was my old stand-by. Wm. Cuthbert. His answer was, 'I do not like to refuse you, but I am too old a man now to go to Fort Lafayette in the winter time, and if you leave the ship and take Tinker with you I know we will be captured.' I said to him, 'I am surprised to hear a man of your intelligence express yourself in that way; what has the dog to do with the safety of the ship? I am ashamed of you.' 'Well, sir, you may call it superstition, or anything you please, but as sure as you leave the ship and take Tinker with you we will be captured.' After considerable persuasion he consented, very unwillingly, to go. 'I'll go in the ship to please you, but I know how it will be.' The ship was captured, and when we met again his first words were: 'I told you so, sir.'*

*I had with me as chief officer an Englishman, who was a very intelligent shipmaster. He was promoted to a command, and when about to try his luck, came to me, saying: 'Captain, let me have Tinker just for one trip and here is five hundred dollars ($500) in gold.' I said: 'Green, two fools, you and I,' but I did not let him have the dog.*[6]

"Dog Tinker" was photographed in Bermuda. Tinker was considered a valuable crew member and a good luck charm by Captain Michael Philip Usina and his crew. Tinker was buried at sea in April 1865. *(Courtesy of Charles V. Peery, MD)*

**M.T. USINA**

Michael Philip Usina was wounded July 21, 1861, at First Manassas while serving with the 8<sup>th</sup> Georgia Infantry. In 1863, Usina was promoted to captain of a blockade runner in the Confederate Navy. *(Courtesy of Charles V. Peery, MD)*

No doubt, Captain Usina considered Tinker not just a mascot, but a valuable member of his crew. Aside from his other duties, Tinker was suspicious of anyone who didn't belong on the ship, and would alert his master whenever a suspicious figure was aboard.[7]

Sadly, Tinker died just after General Robert E. Lee's surrender at Appomattox. Of Tinker's death, Captain Usina says only, "When blockade running ceased, his spirits drooped, his occupation was gone, and he soon sickened and died."[7]

Rather than surrender his command to the Union, Captain Usina sailed for England, turning it over to the one foreign power that might have saved his beloved Confederacy, but did not. En route, "I buried my faithful Tinker among the icebergs of the North Atlantic, and every man on board stood with uncovered head when he was consigned to his watery grave."[8]

*It was one of the saddest moments of my life. The Confederacy, of whose success I had never lost hope, no longer in existence; leaving my native land, as I then thought never more to return; I felt that all the ties that I had formed during my childhood and my youth were become mere memories; that all the fast friends that I had made during our bitter fight, were to be only as some much-loved hero of a favorite novel, with whom we became very familiar until the tale is all told, and who then passes out of our mind and is never heard of more. But it was ordained otherwise, and I am happy now to be in my old home, meeting everywhere men whose sympathies in that grand struggle were the same as my own, and who feel as I do, that though our fighting days are over, the memory of our dead comrades is strong enough to bind us to each other until we all shall be called away to join them in the land of eternal peace.*[9]

# Chapter 8

## An Underage Volunteer

When Congressman Charles Henry Van Wyck began recruiting men from his upstate New York district in the summer of 1861, he envisioned more than just the 56th New York Volunteers, its official designation, but a force worthy of Julius Caesar, the "Tenth Legion." In theory, this legion would comprise two light batteries, two companies of cavalry, a full regiment of infantry and an extra company of sharpshooters made up of boys from the "hill country." Unfortunately, by the time the 10th Legion headed to New York City in November, "a surprising number of recruits took 'French Leave'" (meaning absent without leave). Despite the losses, Van Wyck's legion was still an oversized regiment of 1,130 soldiers[1] soon joined by an underage canine volunteer.

> *. . . The regiment marched down Broadway, which was lined with thousands of people, who cheered and shouted themselves hoarse, and complimented the boys on their good appearance and perfect marching. While marching through Broadway one of the members of Company A picked up a small spotted puppy, which had strayed into the street, and carried it along to Washington, named it Jack, and it remained with the regiment during its entire service, became a special favorite with every member.[2]*

During April 1862, the 56th New York served in the Army of the Potomac as a cog in Major General George B. McClellan's Peninsula Campaign, trying to capture the Confederate capital of Richmond, Virginia.

By the end of May, Gen. McClellan's army had manuevered within 12 miles of Richmond. In fact, the city's soaring church steeples and peeling bells were clearly evident to his forward units. McClellan divided his army, placing two corps south of the Chickahominy River and three to the north. This offered certain advantages to the general, but it became a dangerous deployment because heavy rains had swollen the Chickahominy River, making reinforcement very difficult. Confederate General Joseph E. Johnston wasted no time in exploiting the enemy's weakness. Unfortunately, his complex play fell apart almost immediately on May 31, the first day of the two-day battle at Fair Oaks Station, also known as the battle of Seven Pines or Fair Oaks. But this didn't blunt the terrible carnage inflicted by the Confederate charges against the 56th New York, or the 11th Maine and 52nd Pennsylvania fighting alongside them. With Confederate artillery firing into their front and infantry advancing on their flank, the Federal line was forced to withdraw and re-form on the far side of the "Nine Mile Road," about 300 yards from the Seven Pines.[3]

At one point, while facing infantry attack, an artillery shell ricocheted off an embankment and glanced off Van Wyck's thigh. His scabbard was bent in half, and he had to be carried from the field, though he survived.[4]

*Under tremendous pressure, the Federal line began to give way. Color Sergeant Francis Might of the Tenth Legion boldly stepped forward and waved the flag, bearing the motto 'Our Name is Legion.' He called upon his comrades to rally to the colors. His words and the sight of the flag, by now riddled with bullets, had the desired effect and the line held.*

*'This dreadful contest lasted until nearly dark,' wrote General Henry Naglee, head of the brigade of which the 56th New York was a part. 'My fifty-sixth and One hundred and fourth suffered dreadfully, lost the greater part of their officers and men, and were compelled to give way, carrying their wounded with them.'[5]*

Despite their gallant and orderly retreat in the face of superior numbers on May 31, which contributed to the Confederate's decision to withdraw the next day, McClellan issued a reprimand to Naglee and his superior, alleging that the division had been routed at Fair Oaks. This superior, General Silas Casey, in turn, offered an angry defense of his division:

*In my humble opinion, from what I witnessed on the 31st, I am convinced that the stubborn and desperate resistance of my division saved the army ... from a severe repulse, which might have resulted in a disastrous defeat. The blood of the gallant dead would cry to me from the ground on which they fell fighting for their country had I not said what I have to vindicate them from the unmerited aspersion which has been cast upon them.[6]*

60

Had he been able to make himself understood in English, there's little doubt that Jack would have seconded the General's argument.

*[Jack] was in every skirmish and battle, was wounded in the hip at the battle of Fair Oaks, while sitting on the battle line howling, which was the only time he was touched by balls or shot, and survived all the vicissitudes of camp, bivouac and battle field and returned with the regiment and died of old age.[7]*

**A tintype of an unidentified member of the 56th New York Infantry posing with "Jack."** *(Courtesy of Norm Flayderman)*

This silver collar was a gift to Jack from the regiment. It bore the inscriptions "Jack: the hero of many battles" and "The members of Company A, 56th New York Infantry present this as a lasting memento, feeling confident that could his language be interpreted he would say victory or death." *(Courtesy of Norm Flayderma)*

# Chapter 9

## The Good Soldier

In more recent times, the war dog named Frank might have received a Purple Heart for his valor under fire. He was certainly wounded enough times to qualify. But Frank was a four-legged soldier of the South, and as such, the Confederate canine was technically in rebellion against the nation that would later award that prestigious commendation.

As a puppy, the Newfoundlander volunteered for service with Company B of the 2nd Kentucky Infantry Regiment, which was part of the famous Orphan Brigade, so called because the Kentuckians were driven out of their home state in early 1862, never to return during the course of the war. Frank's origin is not known. He attached himself to a soldier in Company B just before the battle of Fort Donelson, Tennessee. He was a brave canine, but his timing was poor. He was among the 618 men captured after Union forces took the fort on February 16, 1862.[1]

Frank, along with his human comrades, was imprisoned for six months at Camp Morton, Indianapolis, Indiana, until a prisoner exchange was implemented. There, he refused to be tempted by Union soldiers to "jump ship" and join the Yankees, despite repeated offers of food and caresses. When the regiment was marched out from the prison on August 26, 1862, Frank was seen wagging his tail joyfully, departing from his ordinarily dignified demeanor at the prospect of going forth again to "the stern joys of the battle." [2]

Franks' brand of loyalty was often seen among canine mascots attached to soldiers of both Northern and Southern units. Some sociologists might argue that dogs are pack animals that were originally domesticated because they confused certain human beings with alpha dogs, and therefore followed them as they would their canine leaders. But science fails to explain why *some* dogs refused to transfer their affections from one alpha male to another, which many dogs did, especially when coaxed with rewards of food.

Although many stories of canine heroism exist, such behavior was usually the exception to the rule of self-preservation. Most of these pets and mascots were probably not permitted in battle by their owner, hid themselves or ran to the back of the line when sound and sight of musketry and artillery began their human destruction. No one knows why some dogs ignored the perils of war while most had better sense. Perhaps some dogs simply made better soldiers than others.  If so, the temperamental differences seemed to have no connection with breed.

Frank was one of the exceptions.  He relished the sounds of battle, and began a cheering bark when the men around him did.  When they were tense and focused on attacking the enemy, Frank became silent and intent.

*In more than one subsequent engagement he was wounded, but that did not deter him in the least from marching out promptly when the "long roll" was sounded next time, and taking his chances.  If a soldier fell, Frank looked at him with the eye of a philosopher; and the close observer might have discovered something of pity in his glance, and a half-consciousness that the poor man was dead, or in agony, and that he could not help him.  On these, as indeed on almost all occasions, he seemed to partake largely of the spirit of the men.  If the conflict was obstinate, Frank was silent and dogged.  If the men shouted in the onset, or cheered when the ground was won, he barked in unison.*

*On the march he frequently carried his own rations in a small haversack hung on his neck.*

*He almost invariably went out, when not "excused by the surgeon," to company, regimental, and brigade drills, sometimes looking on like a reviewing officer, but oftener taking part in the maneuvers; but he had a sovereign contempt for "dress parade," and generally stayed at his quarters when he found that the men were to go no further than the color-line.*

*He was rather choice, too, in his associates; and, though widely known and friendly to all, he would not allow of much familiarity outside of his own mess.  When rations were short, he would visit other messes, and even other companies, and accept the little that his friends could spare; but he did not want them to presume upon his sense of obligation, and indulge in anything like caresses.*

*In this way he lived the soldier's life.  If Co. B had a shelter, Frank had his corner in it.  When he was shot, his wounds were dressed, and he had no lack of attention.  If the commissariat were well supplied, he fed bountifully, and put on his best looks.  If life were eked out on "hard-tack" and a slice of bacon, or of poor beef, Frank had but his share of that, and grew lean and hollow-eyed, like his soldier-friends.* [3]

On one occasion, Frank was injured, not by Union bullets, but by a fellow Confederate canine. The battle of dog vs. dog was part of a famous snowball fight that took place in Dalton, Georgia, between the men of the 2$^{nd}$ Kentucky and their compatriots. When everyone woke up on March 22, 1864, they discovered that three or four inches of snow had fallen, and proceeded to pelt each other with the fluffy stuff and to maneuver as if they were engaged in actual combat. One soldier, Private John S. Jackman of the 9$^{th}$ Kentucky Infantry in the Orphan Brigade, described the fracas in terms that a military historian would appreciate. His recollections offer a rare glimpse into how ordinary soldiers would sometimes amuse themselves.

> *Last night the snow fell three or four inches deep, and continued snowing, not very hard though, through the day. We have seen more fun to-day than at any one time during the war. Early in the morning, the 4$^{th}$ Ky., whose camp is near Tyler's brigade of our division, got up a snow fight with Tyler's men, and all the other regiments in our brigade went to reinforce the 4$^{th}$. After fighting awhile, our brigade and Tyler's "made friends" and both went over to Finley's Fla. Brigade of our division, and charged the camp. Finley was soon "cleaned out."*
>
> *Not having seen enough fun, our division (Bates) marched on Stovall's brigade, Stewart's division, two miles off. We marched in military order, and when we got in the neighborhood of the camp, sent forward, after forming lines of battle, a line of skirmishers to develop the enemy. Our skirmishers soon had to fall back before superior numbers, and we made a general assault. We took the camp with so little fighting—not having seen near sport enough—our lines fell back, and let Stovall's men prepare for defense. By this time, Gen'l S came in person, and had his brigade formed. We charged again, and took a stand of colors, and Gen'l S. himself. Lt. McC., and myself had the honor to capture the flag, which we brought to camp. Having entirely demoralized Stovall, we came home. I got several bruises.*[4]

Unfortunately for Frank, this mock fight was to be one of his last. In the summer campaign of 1864, he disappeared.[5] The men of the 2$^{nd}$ Kentucky hoped that he had simply run away or been taken in and cared for by either the enemy or another Confederate regiment.

Having been captured with Company B of the 2nd Kentucky at Fort Donelson early in 1862, Frank missed the battle of Shiloh in April. But an unsigned article appearing in the 1882 "Southern Bivouac," tells the story of another dog in Frank's Orphan Brigade, a pup, which unfortunately was at Shiloh:

*A member of Company H, Fourth Kentucky Regiment, owned a pup which followed him into the battle of Shiloh. The second day of the fight, the writer of this observed the faithful creature sitting on his haunches in the rear of the company, and on a line with the file closers. We were engaged in supporting Cobb's battery, and it seemed that the whole North had suddenly concentrated their stock of powder and iron and were determined to plow us up and turn us under. The dog sat there, and viewing him as I was lying flat on the ground, it seemed the missiles shook his ears by their close proximity to his head. He was struck by and by and as I never saw him again I think he was killed. I can never forget the seeming anxiety depicted on his countenance while we were getting shelled, but faithful to the instincts of his race, this little long-eared puppy remained near his master, till the piece of iron ended his existence.*[6]

The 2nd Kentucky Infantry was among the last to surrender in the East, on April 26, 1865, along with the Army of Tennessee.[7] The remainder of the Orphan Brigade laid down their arms in the first week of May 1865 at Washington, Georgia, nearly a month after Lee surrendered at Appomattox. Only 500 members of the original 4,000 soldiers of the Brigade remained.

A dog pictured with Captain Frederick Barton and non-commissioned officers of Co. E, 10th Massachusetts Infantry taken at Camp Brightwood, Washington, DC, in August 1861. *(Massachusetts MOLLUS Collection. Army Military History Institute)*

This unique carte de visite of a dog with a kepi and pipe bears the following inscription on the back: "Henry Ulke, 278 Pennsylvania Avenue, Washington, D. C. 1865." Ulke moved to Washington in 1860, and opened a photography and portrait studio. He was living at Petersen House, across from Ford's Theater, when Lincoln was brought there after being shot. *(Author's Collection)*

# Chapter 10

## Deathless Love

The battle of Shiloh, or Pittsburg Landing, was fought in southwestern Tennessee on April 6-7, 1862, not far from the Mississippi border. Summarizing the results of the battle, historian Shelby Foote wrote:

> *Of the 100,000 soldiers engaged in this first great bloody conflict of the war, approximately one out of every four who had gone into battle had been killed, wounded or captured. Casualties were 24 percent, the same as Waterloo's. Yet Waterloo had settled something, while this one apparently had settled nothing. When it was over the two armies were back where they started, with other Waterloos ahead. In another sense, however, it had settled a great deal. The American volunteer, whichever side he was on in this war, and however green, would fight as fiercely and stand as firmly as the vaunted veterans of Europe.*[1]

Among these fierce-fighting volunteers, and among those killed, was a thirty-something German immigrant Geometer, a mathematician specializing in geometry, from Illinois named Louis W. Pfeif.[2] Lieutenant Pfeif and his dog, whose name has been lost to history, joined the 58th Illinois Infantry Volunteers at Camp Douglas, Chicago, in the winter of 1862. On February 12, he and his regiment of 887 men headed south to Kentucky and Tennessee.[3]

Recently promoted for his capture of Fort Donelson, Tennessee, Major General Ulysses S. Grant was caught off guard when Confederate General Albert Sidney Johnston marched his army north to trap Grant's forces on a small plain surrounded on three sides by the Tennessee River and two small creeks. The surprise was almost inexplicable, since Johnston's forces had been delayed for several days by poor coordination and bad weather, and some of the rebel soldiers, worried their powder had gotten damp, test-fired their muskets within earshot of the Federals and gave the rebel yell.[4]

One Union colonel nearly became unstrung, certain he was about to be attacked en masse, but Grant and a cautious William Tecumseh Sherman thought he was merely crying wolf.

On the morning of April 6, Lieutenant Pfeif and his comrades of the 58th Illinois Infantry was near a division commanded by General Benjamin M. Prentiss. Pfeif had brought along his pet dog, and one can only imagine the poor canine's reaction when Confederate artillery opened up on the surprised Union infantry that morning, and eager battle lines of Confederates began streaming toward them.

Repulsed by the initial onslaught, Prentiss' division fell back across an open field until they came to an eroded wagon trail that wound along the edge of heavy woods. Here they decided to make a stand, in the shallow natural trench of a sunken road, just as Grant arrived.

"Maintain that position at all hazards," Grant told Prentiss.

Prentiss said he would try. And he did.[5]

For about six hours, Union soldiers blasted away at wave after wave of charging Confederates while the other divisions on their flanks were forced to retreat. By evening, the 2,200 survivors of Prentiss' division, well under half the number he had started with that morning, were forced to surrender to the Confederates or face annihilation.[6]

But the time Prentiss' division had bought for the rest of the army was precious, allowing reinforcements to begin coming up that evening. Next day, Johnston's army was forced back to Corinth, Mississippi, their starting point nearly a week before.

There is no record of how Pfeif died, only that he *did* die during the battle, leaving behind his wife Eliz and Louisa, age five.[7] According to soldiers who had been nearby, when Lieutenant Pfeif fell, his faithful dog was by his side and remained there, licking his wounds until he was taken from the field and buried.

*A faithful dog.—The widow of Lieut. Pfeif, of Illinois, was enabled to find her husbands grave, at Pittsburg Landing, by seeing a dog which had accompanied the Lieutenant to the war. The dog approached her with the most intense manifestations of joy, and immediately indicated to her, as well as he was able, his desire that she should follow him. She did so, and he led the way to a distant part of the field, and stopped before a single grave. She caused it to be opened, and there found the body of her dead husband. It appears from the statements of some of the soldiers, that when Lieut. Pfeif fell, his dog was by his side, and thus remained, licking his wounds, until he was taken from the field and buried. He then took his station by the grave, and nothing could induce him to abandon it, but for a sufficient length of time each day to satisfy his hunger, until, by some means, he was made aware of the presence of his mistress. Thus he watched for twelve days by the grave of his slain master.* [8]

**Union soldiers and a dog enjoy the view from Lookout Mountain, Tennessee.** *(Author's Collection)*

**Corporal Levi Hubbard of Company B, 35<sup>th</sup> New York Infantry, with his mailbag and dog.** (*Author's Collection*)

# Chapter 11

## Dash, the Firedog

From 1856 to 1861, Dash was the firedog of the Good Will Fire Company in Philadelphia, where the only known photo of him was taken in 1859, one of the earliest canine images ever captured by the new medium.[1] Dash appears to have been a Standard Poodle, whose earliest ancestors were probably curly-coated dogs from central Asia that assisted with herding animals.

On August 11, 1861, Dash was mustered in by men of the 23rd Pennsylvania Infantry, most of whom belonged to one of 96 fire companies in and around Philadelphia.[2] The regiment came to be called Birney's Zouaves, after their commander, David Bell Birney, a prominent Philadelphia lawyer and businessman whose father was once the anti-slavery candidate for the Presidency of the Liberty Party. The Zouaves (pronounced *zoo-AHVs*) of the Union Army were typified by baggy pants—often red , white/tan leggings or gaiters, a short trimmed  jacket, and a tasseled red fez , making them look more like soldiers of the French Army than American fighting men.

On September 8, 1861, Dash and the regiment arrived at Camp Graham, about three miles north of Washington, DC. The regiment camped there through mid-March 1862, during which they were carefully instructed, drilled and disciplined by Colonel Birney.

Of course, not all their time was spent learning to become soldiers, since the average age of the men at that time was only nineteen. There was still time for baseball, sack races, ox roasting, pig races, boxing, pole climbing and the whirligig for prizes. Day by day, the regimental band also lifted the spirits of the men by playing patriot songs.[3] During the time in camp, Dash may have been the only Civil War canine to have seen President Abraham Lincoln in person, on two different occasions.

On November 8, the 23rd formed part of a brigade of about 12,000 men.  Each man received 20 rounds of blank cartridge and marched to an open field a mile from Washington. General McClellan, President Lincoln, and a number of distinguished officers reviewed them as the band struck up "Hail to the Chief."  After the review, the brigade drilled all day, and then marched back to camp.[4]

Another opportunity for Dash to have seen the President occurred when Secretary of War Simon Cameron requested that the regiment march to Washington and parade down Pennsylvania Avenue.  With

15 companies, 1,427 strong, a band of 36 pieces and a drum corps of 30 pieces, the regiment made quite a display, and it was heartily applauded all along the route.[5] It was not uncommon at this time for a regimental mascot or pet to participate in such an important review or parade.

During the time camped near Washington, DC, late August 1861, to his participation in the Peninsula Campaign, March-June 1862, Dash gained a considerable amount of weight. In fact, he put on so many pounds that he couldn't keep up during marches, so various men took turns carrying him. Dash seemed to know all the men, was well loved, and they shared too many of their rations with him.

In the advance of the Army of the Potomac on the Virginia Peninsular, spring of 1862, the 23rd Pennsylvania would have its first encounter with the Confederates at Warwick River, where they lost one man. They came under Confederate fire again during the siege of Yorktown, the battle of Williamsburg, Bottoms Bridge, and then on a reconnaissance mission four miles outside of Richmond. The regiment was not heavily engaged, nor did they take serious casualties during these early encounters with the Confederates, but their honor and bravery were well tested, and they gave a good account of themselves under enemy fire. They also discovered that Dash, their fire-dog, seemed to be in his element while under fire. Their mettle was soon tested again, however, and their early engagements could not have fully prepared them for what was about to come.

In the afternoon and evening of May 30, Dash and the 23rd Pennsylvania were near the front of the advancing Army. Moving toward Richmond, the weather turned violent, with thunderstorms passing and re-passing over their march and then their camps. Rains filled the creeks, slowing the army's advance.[6] On the next day, the battle of Fair Oaks began. For Dash and the men, the thunderstorms from the previous day must have seemed mild compared to what they would experience this day.

Not long after noon, as most of the regiment finished eating their first meal, a single piece of Confederate artillery fired a six-pound solid shot that struck open the ground to the left and front of the camp. Shortly after, the sounds of battle increased to the front of their camp and the men of the 23rd moved instinctively, as well trained soldiers, and took their place in line without knapsacks, canteens, or haversacks. Colonel Birney had been promoted to Brigadier General, so Colonel Thomas Neill led the Zouaves into battle. Neill quickly moved the regiment into position and then formed them into a battle line.[7]  The Reverend. James G. Shinn, chaplain of the regiment, described what happened during this early scene of the battle:

> *As the line of the 23d was forming, at the instant that the color guard stepped to the front of the regiment, Color Sergeant Samuel Bolton, a good and brave soldier, fell struck by a rifle-ball directly in the forehead. Though sick that day and not fit for duty, yet, rather than give room for even the slightest suspicion of cowardice or unfaithfulness, he stood nobly at his post of duty, even though he knew that post of duty was a post of imminent peril.[8]*

Color Sergeant Samuel Bolton was the first of three regimental color bearers shot down that day. During the battle, the 23rd drove the enemy from their positions with several successful bayonet charges. Late in the afternoon, they were ferociously counter-attacked, and the regiment barely escaped capture by an enemy column that swept down in their rear.  Colonel Neill continued to lead his men, even after his horse was shot out from under him.

The men of the 23rd Pennsylvania suffered great losses.  Seven officers and 136 men were killed or wounded.[9]  Several others were captured or went missing that day. Among the wounded and captured, but not listed in the official numbers, was Dash.

As evening arrived, the men of Birney's Zouaves must have pondered the fate of their missing and lost comrades. No doubt, Dash was on the minds of some. On the following day, Private Ed Rehn of Company B wrote this in his diary:

> *June 1 1862*
> *Dash was captured by the rebels yesterday with some of the boys from Co. B. Shinn and Hildebrand are among those missing. We have fallen back from yesterday's fight and are awaiting orders.[10]*

On June 1, the battle resumed, but the regiment was ordered to march with General Innis Palmer's command on a reconnaissance to White Oak Swamp.  The following day, it returned to find its camp destroyed and all articles of value lost.[11]  To the survivors, the previous days must have seemed long and full of great sorrow. With the loss of so many friends, their camp and personal items in it destroyed, the men were in need of some good news. This news arrived when it was learned that Dash, Chaplain Shinn and a few others had made their way back to the regiment.

Private Rehn wrote in his diary:

*June 3 1862*
*Some of Company B has been sent to Libby. A few of the men escaped as did Dash. He has been wounded several times. One of the boys found him on the retreat away from Fair Oaks Station. Throughout the day he has received quite a bit of attention from the regiment. Dash was as brave as any soldier in Battle and took a rebel bullet in the side. We will at our earliest opportunity send him home a hero.*[12]

The decision to honorably discharge Dash and ship him home to the Delaware Engine House in Philadelphia was due in part to the wounds he suffered in battle. In addition, thanks to the men's affections administered in the form of food, Dash's weight became too much for the dog to bear. He was no longer fit for duty.

William Wray's account of Dash is recorded in the regimental history, and reads as follows:

*The Twenty-third Philadelphia had a fire-dog called "Dash"; he seemed to know all the boys and was in his element when under fire. At Fair Oaks he and the chaplain were captured, but during the night both got back to the lines. "Dash" becoming too fat to keep up on the march, the boys took turns at carrying him. He was wounded, honorably discharged and shipped to the Delaware Engine House, where he belonged. He never reached there, however, as he was lost on the way up from the front.*[13]

Somewhere between The Virginia Peninsula and Philadelphia, Dash was lost and never seen again. Once again, the men of Birney's Zouaves would ponder the fate of a lost friend, but this time, no answers were ever forthcoming.

The war continued for the 23rd Pennsylvania Volunteers, and as it did, many more were lost. The regiment was engaged in battles that included Malvern Hill, Fredericksburg, Banks' Ford, Gettysburg and Cold Harbor. At Cold Harbor, they suffered their greatest losses of the war.

After the war, the regiment formed the Survivor's Association of The Twenty-third Pennsylvania Volunteers, composed of honorably discharged men from the 23<sup>rd</sup> Pennsylvania Volunteer Infantry and those transferred from the 23<sup>rd</sup>.[14]  Along with their activities and good works, the organization often held meetings and annual reunions.  The First Annual Reunion of The Survivor's Association was held at Maennerchor Hall, Philadelphia, on May 31, 1882, the 20<sup>th</sup> anniversary of Fair Oaks.  After dinner that evening, Chaplain Shinn delivered his review of the battle.

Although he did not mention Dash in his review, it's likely that Shinn and the other survivors had Dash on their minds that night and talked about their memories of him, a dog that seemed to know all the boys and was in his element under fire, a canine as brave as any human being, Dash the Firedog.

This Image of "Dash the Firedog" was taken by commercial photographer Isaac A. Rehn, Philadelphia, 1859. Before the war, Dash was the firedog at the "Delaware Engine House" in Philadelphia. *(Life of the 23rd Pennsylvania "Birney's Zouaves" Civil War, Reissued Lisa Wray Mazzanti 1999, 2003. Courtesy of 23rd Pennsylvania Re-enactor Frank P. Marrone, Jr.)*

An unidentified Zouave and civilian pictured with a small dog at their feet that is alert to movement outside the range of the camera. The Zouave's uniform is complete with baggy trousers, sash, Zouave jacket and fez, which is wrapped with a white turban. The sash has been tinted red. Over his shoes he is wearing a pair of leather leggings, or they may just be boots. *(Author's Collection)*

Civil War Veteran with his dog in the 1890's.

The back of this photo identifies the man: "Mr. Crane, Upper Powow St., Amesbury, Mass. Civil War Veteran." The shadow is that of Etta Woodman, Winter St., Amesbury.

William Crane was a 28-year-old Painter living in Amesbury, Massachusetts when he enlisted as a private in Company E of the 1st Massachusetts Heavy Artillery on July 5, 1861. He was later promoted to corporal, and mustered out of service on July 8, 1864. After the war, Crane was a member of Grand Army of the Republic (GAR) Post #117 (Moses Ellis) in Medfield, Massachusetts. He died on October 6, 1912. *(Author's Collection)*

# Chapter 12

## Dog Jack's Silver Collar

Not every canine mascot was warmly welcomed by his human comrades. Such is the case of the stray Bull Terrier that was later named Jack, known also as Dog Jack by the soldiers of the 102nd Regiment of Pennsylvania Volunteers. Sometime before the war, the black and white dog wandered into the Niagara Volunteer Fire Engine House on Pennsylvania Avenue in Pittsburgh. He was initially ignored by the firefighters. In fact, some of the men considered him such a nuisance that on one occasion, Jack was kicked so hard that one of his legs was broken. Fortunately, some of the firefighters took pity on Jack, put his fractured leg in splints, and nursed him back to health.[1]

Opinions toward Jack remained divided in the firehouse until Jack proved his mettle. When a much larger dog attacked Jack, a spark was ignited. He'd had enough of all this bullying, and he fought with a vengeance. This was no minor quarrel; this was revenge for all the abuse this little Bull Terrier had suffered in his short lifetime, for every growl, kick, and unkind word he had ever borne; for every abuse that had ever been heaped on this stray's broken body. If he died, he didn't intend to go in disgrace.

That fire within served him well. Jack was the victor; his reward was the affection of every Niagara fireman. Having been adopted as the company's mascot, Jack raced along with his human companions toward scenes of devastation whenever the fire alarm was sounded.[2]

It's no surprise, therefore, that when the Niagara fire company enlisted *en masse* in the 102nd Pennsylvania Infantry, they brought along "a doleful black-and-white Bull Terrier named Jack, whose subsequent career spanned nearly all of the regiment's battles in Virginia and Maryland."[3] With most of his firemen friends enlisting in Company F of the 102nd Pennsylvania, Jack swore allegiance to the regiment. It was said that he understood bugle calls and followed only the men of his own regiment, and that after a battle he brought relief to the wounded and searched out the dead of his regiment on the field.[4]

Chaplain of the 102nd Pennsylvania Infantry, Alexander M. Stewart, in his book *March and Battlefield: or Three Years with the Army of the Potomac*, tells another story of how Jack joined the firefighters in Pittsburgh:

PHOTO
ADDIS-WASH. D.C.
1865

"DOG JACK"
102d REG. PENNA. VOLS.

"Dog Jack" of the 102$^{nd}$ Pennsylvania Infantry. Before the war, Jack was the mascot of the Niagara Volunteer Fire Engine House in Pittsburgh, Pennsylvania. (*History of the Pittsburgh Washington Infantry, 102nd (Old 13th Regiment), Pennsylvania Veteran Volunteers and Its Forbearers, 1931.*)

*Once, upon a dark night, in the city of Pittsburgh the Niagara fire-engine was being boisterously hurried along a narrow street, in order to extinguish some rising flame or imagined combustion. Out of a dark alley came a young puppy, evidently much alarmed at the clamor, and by his vigorous barking, seeming vainly to imagine he could put a stop to such a noisy tumult. A rather natural result followed. The engine ran over puppy's leg and broke it. Though noisy, and sometimes charged with rowdyism, yet are members of fire companies not devoid of kindly sympathies. The loud howlings of puppy over his injury, soon brought one of the boys to his relief, by whom lie was carried to the engine-house, and the leg splintered, which in time healed. Puppy soon became a favorite with the boys, got JACK as a cognomen [surname], grew up beside the engine, and eventually became a large, fine-looking, tri-colored mastiff. Jack was always in high glee when the fire-bell sounded, ran with the shouting company, and rendered all the assistance possible.*

*Ere long the times changed. The rebellion broke out, and many of the Niagara engine boys were enlisting. Jack listened with all due attention to the various discussions held thereat in the engine-house, and soon got it into his doggish head that something unusual was in the wind. As he walked about in a dignified manner, all the while*
> *"His gourie tail, wi' upward curl,*
> *Hung o'er his hurdies wi' a swurl, "*

*and with an occasional bow-wow—all of which signified, that if any big fire was to be extinguished, Jack was one to help. Starting-time came, and sure enough, Jack was amongst the first to enter the ears. Although he did not take the oath of allegiance, yet none the less true has he proved himself. He became enrolled in company A, which leads the regiment. Jack leads the company, thus being always ahead, whether on parade, the march, or battle-field.*[5]

Among the problems with this narrative, of course, is the fact that Jack was a Bull Terrier, not a Mastiff. In my attempt to represent the true facts about Civil War canines, it would be unfair to both you and Jack if I did not mention that accounts differ as to what happened to Jack at the battle of Malvern Hill July 1, 1862. Chaplain Stewart recorded this defense of Jack:

> *A slanderous report was indeed put into circulation, that at the fearful battle of Malvern Hills, when shot and shell, canister and Minnie began to fall thick and fast, Jack skedaddled, and rejoined his company after the fray was over. This is, however, by many flatly denied, so that Jack claims the benefit of the demurrer. His broken bone not having been set according to science, the leg, in consequence, remains crooked. It hence often gets hurt—where at Jack will hold it up for inspection or sympathy, in a manner quite creditable to any limping soldier in one of our numerous hospitals.*[6]

John H. Niebaum, in his 1931 regimental history of the 102nd Pennsylvania Infantry, *History of the Pittsburgh Washington Infantry, 102nd (Old 13th Regiment),* gives us this of Jack at the battle:

*He was wounded at Malvern Hill, being shot through the shoulder and back, for many days he hovered between life and death and his sufferings brought tears to his sorrowing comrades.*

*The Medical Corps of the regiment did all for him that science could suggest for his recovery, at the Hospital tent.*

*When he recovered and took to the field he was greeted by the hearty cheers of the regiment.[7]*

Perhaps some of the confusion for our sources is that according to Chaplain Stewart, the 102nd Pennsylvania had at least two more dogs. There was Beauty that was killed by a bursting-shell at Malvern Hill,[8] and York, who became acquainted with Jack on more than one occasion, during the march.

*The-other dog [York] is a curious-looking specimen of the canine. One must be more skilled in doggery than the writer, to define his species. Spaniel, cur, terrier, and water-dog all seem blended in one.*

*Volunteering in the regiment while encamped in the city of York, Pa., in May, 1861, he is, in accordance, surnamed York. He is enrolled in company B, which occupies the extreme left or rear of the regiment. Should Jack at any time approach the rear, every hair on York's body is at once on end. Should York approach the right, Jack sends him back according to true military style and authority.*

*Marvelous stories are told by the boys concerning the experience and knowledge in military affairs acquired by these dogs; all of which, if written, would fill a volume, and put to shame many a Brigadier.*

*Two years have now elapsed since the above chronicle was made of our two camp friends. These two eventful years have made rapid and fearful changes among the human members of our regiment, as well as of the whole army. Nor have our canine companions been exceptions to war's rapid mutations. Eighteen months since, poor York sank under a complication of injuries, diseases and exposures—died in camp, was buried with appropriate military honors by the members of his company, while a board at the spot duly chronicles the event.[9]*

For better or worse, the men of the 102nd Pennsylvania did not fret over saving face during combat. They were engaged in the bloodiest battles of Virginia and Maryland. These men worried about staying *alive* through battles that included the siege of Yorktown, Savage's Station, Malvern Hill, Antietam, Fredericksburg, Marye's Heights, Salem Church, Gettysburg, Wilderness, Spotsylvania, Cold Harbor, 1st Petersburg, siege at Petersburg, Fort Stevens, Winchester, Fishers Hill, Cedar Creek, Fort Steadman, Appomattox and any number of unnamed skirmishes.[10] The 102nd Pennsylvania was nearly everywhere in the eastern theater of the war.

In May 1863, the regiment ran up against the Confederates at Salem Church, Virginia.

> *The Corps formed line of battle, our brigade being on the extreme right, and the fight was on, lasting until 6:00 P. M., when we were moved from the right to the center to strengthen it for an attack in force by the "Rebs." Late in the evening, the most of the troops were moved off to Banks Ford. No orders were received by the regiment and we were astounded to see and hear the Johnnies coming at us from all sides, crying for us to "surrender," and "what you all doing here anyways."*
>
> *We were to be sacrificed to save the balance of the Corps. As it was, 94 officers and men, not including Dog Jack, were gathered in by Wilcox's Georgia Brigade, the balance of the regiment getting out safely. This was where we lost our Colors, not taken in the fight but found by the "Rebs," where someone had thought they had hidden them while they were getting away from Wilcox's Georgians.[11]*

During the battle of Salem Church, Dog Jack was captured by the Confederates and made a prisoner of war until the fall of 1863 when he was exchanged for a *human* Confederate soldier, so much did Jack's compatriots think of him. Or perhaps his Confederate jailers also thought highly of Jack.

> *He was captured by the enemy at Salem Church, Va., May 3rd, 1863, and was exchanged for a Confederate soldier at Belle Isle, Va., and returned to the regiment in the fall of 1863, having been a prisoner for six months. During the engagement at Savage Station [actually Cedar Creek], he was again captured, but after being detained about six hours he managed to escape and returned to the Union lines. While in prison at Belle Isle, Jack's presence and popularity cheered the Union prisoners.[12]*

85

Members of the 102nd Pennsylvania, while in Pittsburgh in August 1864, gave a silver collar to Dog Jack. While on veteran furlough, they held a ball at Lafayette Hall and raised $75.00, using the money to buy a silver collar and medal for "Jack." [13]

Unfortunately, this precious gift may have sealed Dog Jack's fate. On December 23, 1864, at Frederick City, Maryland, Jack disappeared. Although no one knows what really happened to Jack, some speculate that he died fighting to keep his silver collar from the hands of robbers. The general conclusion by the men of the regiment was that Jack was killed by a mercenary for the value of the silver collar which he had always worn.[14] Whatever the case, neither Jack nor the silver collar was ever seen again. The Soldiers and Sailors National Military Museum & Memorial in Pittsburgh would like to add this historic artifact to their collection and tribute to Dog Jack, a true hero of the Civil War.

**A rare view of "Dog Jack" wearing his silver collar.**
*(Author's Collection)*

This image of Dog Jack was found in a family photo album that belonged to Margaret Keifer the wife of Private Andrew S. Keifer. During the war Keifer served in the 70th New York Infantry and in the Veteran Reserve Corps. Both Keifer and Dog Jack lived in the Pittsburgh, Pennsylvania, area before the war. *(Author's Collection)*

"Our Dog Jack on Guard" for the 102$^{nd}$ Pennsylvania Infantry. During the war Dog Jack and 94 of his human comrades were taken prisoner at the battle of Salem Church. After six months as a Prisoner of War at Belle Isle Virginia, Jack was exchanged for a Confederate soldier. *(Author's Collection)*

# Chapter 13

## Charlie & Robert Lee

*Permit me to pay a loving tribute to a little comrade who often cheered our hearts by his winning ways and shared all of our privations and dangers…. At Staunton in the afternoon of August 1 [1861] a little friend came into our camp who made himself sociable with the boys. He was small and uncouth, but showed a genial disposition, and he soon won the friendship of the company. He was invited to spend the night, and a bountiful supper and comfortable bed were given him. The next day when we took up the line of march, he signified his desire to become an independent member of the company, and was cordially accepted. From that day until Appomattox he was faithful and fondly petted by every member.*

*He endured fatigue and privation without a murmur, participated in every battle in which the company engaged, and was always in the front rank, where the shells and bullets fell the thickest. He seemed to enjoy the whistling of bullets, shrieking of shells, and to go wild with delight as the combat raged. He was too small to take an active part in the work, but would dart back and forth from gun to gun, cheering the men with his clear, ringing voice, which could be heard distinctly above the din of the battle. In the body of this little four-legged comrade beat a warm, affectionate heart.*

*We named him "Charlie."*[1]

The company to which Charlie attached himself was originally organized in Athens, Georgia, in 1858 as the National Artillery. Shortly after Georgia seceded from the Union, they changed their name to the Troup Artillery in honor of the state's former Governor, George M. Troup. Afterward, they were sometimes known as Carlton's Battery for their captain, Henry Hull Carlton. Within weeks after the fall of Fort Sumter on April 14, 1861, the men of the Troup Artillery were on their way north, first to Savannah and then to Richmond, where they arrived in early July and "named their guns in honor of the patriotic citizens of Athens."[2]

They were then ordered to western Virginia, and it was at Staunton that Charlie wandered into their camp, no doubt in search of a good meal and warm companionship. We are not quite certain what Charlie looked like or what his breed was. In *Confederate Veteran Magazine*, George B. Atkisson, who had served with the Troup Artillery as a private, merely said, "He was not very pretty, and boasted no illustrious pedigree."[3]

The Troup Artillery may have had another mascot, named Robert Lee, who was sometimes confused with Charlie by Robert Stiles of the Richmond Howitzer, who later recounted the various exploits of these dogs:

*There were two little dogs in the battalion which afforded not only a good deal of amusement, but also a field for some interesting observation and discrimination. Both were small, the Troup Artillery dog, the larger of the two, about the size of a small coon without a tail, which he in general resembled. He was dark, stone gray on his back, inclining (somewhat more than a coon) to tan or fawn color underneath. He had also rough, coarse hair; short, stout legs, and, as implied, little or no tail. He had entered the service early, joining the battery during the unfortunate campaign in Western Virginia, and was named after the commanding general, "Robert Lee." He was very plucky in a personal difficulty, but I blush to say, an abject coward in battle.*

*[During the battle of Chancellorsville]... my eye chanced to light upon poor little Bob Lee sneaking to the rear, in fright absolutely pitiable. It may serve as an excuse for him that he had gotten separated from his company, which had been left behind at Fredericksburg with Early. To my astonishment, he made for a large tree, back of which and as close in and under as possible he crept, and crouched and squatted, very much as a demoralized man might have done. The action and the purpose were unmistakable. I do not know that I could have believed it if I had not seen it with my own eyes, but there was no room for doubt. One might not feel generously and sympathetically inclined toward a man under such circumstances, but it is pleasant to be able to say that little Bob's prudent precautions accomplished their object. As I have always understood, he passed safely through the war and followed the men of his battery to Georgia.[4]*

The physical description of the dog named Robert Lee fits with Atkisson's meager portrait of Charlie, but obviously the name is different. What is more, Atkisson says that Charlie demonstrated unparalleled courage under fire, and unlike Robert Lee, Charlie did not pass safely through the war to follow his men back home.

Given the reckless bravery displayed by some soldiers of the Troup Artillery at Yorktown and Fredericksburg, for example, it's doubtful they would have heaped as much praise as they did on Charlie had he shown the kind of cowardice displayed by Robert Lee.

*At the battle of Fredericksburg a shell fell behind the breastworks where our battery was. The fuse of the shell was sputtering and burning. All fell to the ground to escape the explosion, but Dick Saye ran to it and, bravely picking up the dangerous shell, threw it over the breastworks, where it immediately exploded without doing any harm. If this had been done by a Federal soldier, he would have received a medal of honor, which is given only for distinguished acts of bravery.*

*Another heroic member of the Troup Artillery, [was] Bill Mealer. ... At Dam No. 1, near Yorktown, a cannon ball struck Bill on the leg below the knee. The lower part was held on by a small piece of the skin. Bill coolly took out his pocketknife and cut the skin in two and threw the foot and ankle away, saying: "D—— you, you never was any account, anyhow." Bill afterwards served in the cavalry although having but one good leg. That was pluck for you.[5]*

As told by Atkisson, Charlie's exploits nearly rivaled those of his human companions:

*When we crossed the Potomac in the Maryland campaign [September 6, 1862], Charlie was placed on the foremost caisson for safety, the river being too wide and swift for him to swim. As the horses reached the shore, Charlie sprang to the ground, the first one of the company to reach "Maryland, My Maryland." Here he danced and barked with delight till the last gun had crossed, and then gravely took up the line of march with the company. At Sharpsburg [September 17, 1862] Charlie was in his glory. He ran up and down the line from gun to gun. He would wiggle his little body with joy, while his bark rang out with the roar of battle. He seemed not to know fear, and as the battle grew fiercer so did his joy. At Fredericksburg, Gettysburg, Spotsylvania, and in every engagement he was always present and always exhibiting the same wild joy and courage.*

When General Lee held the grand review of the Army of Northern Virginia at Brandy Station, Va., prior to the Pennsylvania campaign, Charlie was given the seat of honor upon one of the caissons, and as he passed was honored be a grave salute from the general commanding. Charlie acknowledged the honor by a wiggle of his body (he had no tail to wag) and a loud bark. Charlie was well known to the men of Longstreet's Corps, and frequent effort was made to steal him from us; but he was true to his "first love," and in a few days would find his way back to our camp to be hailed with joy.

Charlie was a good forager, and many a rabbit fell a victim to his hunting prowess, to say nothing of a few stray chickens. He brought his game into camp, giving it impartially. During the Maryland campaign he strictly obeyed General Lee's orders, refusing to leave the ranks. When some of the boys would say, "Charlie, go bring us a chicken." He would pay no attention, but jog along with the guns. He looked upon people in Maryland as friends, and refused to steal from them. On the Pennsylvania campaign however, he changed his ideas; being on the enemy's soil, he plundered. Many a "Dutch wife" lost her chickens and complained: "Captain, von little dog vot pelongs to your company steal mine chickens and bring dem to your mens. I vants my chickens, or you pay for them." The captain would reply: "Well my friend, point out the men with the dog and I will see that you get your chickens or they will be paid for." Among so many men it was impossible to point out the right ones.

During the last months of the Confederacy rations were cooked at camps located at a safe distance. Charlie spent most of his time at the guns, but always went to the camp for his meals. At meal time some one would say: "Charlie, go hurry up dinner." With a wise look he would dart off to the camp and make his errand known to the cooks by loud barks and wiggling of his body. If all was ready, the cooks would say: "All right, Charlie, here we go," and away they went, Charlie showing his joy by barking and dancing around the bearer's heels. If meals were not ready, the cook would say: "Go back and tell the boys it will be an hour yet before dinner *is ready." With a sorrowful look he would sneak back and quietly curl himself up in a dark corner, and the boys knew what it meant. After a while some would say: "Charlie, go and bring dinner," but he would not move. At the end of his hour he would go back to camp. "All right, Charlie, dinner is ready; let us go." Then his spirit would revive.*

*Now we come to the last scene. Petersburg is abandoned and the line of the retreat is taken up. Not an hour is passed without a rain of shells and bullets. Two days before the surrender* [April 7, 1865, the battle of Cumberland Church] *in a slight engagement a shell struck a tree by which Charlie was standing and exploded, and when the smoke cleared away little Charlie was dead. His grave was dug at the foot of a tree and the body of our faithful "comrade" was consigned to his last resting place. I can safely write that there was not a dry eye among that group of war-worn veterans as the dirt hid from view his little body. Rest in peace, little comrade! For nearly four years you were our faithful companion and loving pet. You shared our dangers and our pleasures. While your moldering body lies beneath Virginia's sod, your memory is yet fresh and green in the hearts of every surviving member of the Troup Artillery, Carlton's Battery. I fondly fancy that the trees cast a loving shade, that the winter winds wail less mournfully, and the wild flowers blossom more lovingly over your little grave.*[6]

**A Civil War period photo of a dog in a chair.**
*(Author's Collection)*

# Chapter 14

## Bob, the Preacher's Dog

Not all men who served in the Civil War carried guns into the fray. Support personnel such as surgeons, sutlers and chaplains all played important roles, too. One soldier who fought for God's side was the Right Reverend Arthur Edwards, who tended the spiritual needs of the 1st Michigan Infantry. Edwards even brought his own support staff in the form of a friendly dog named Bob.

The 1st Michigan Infantry, like so many of the Union's Civil War units, was first organized for a term of three-months and it came together on April 24, 1861, in Detroit. By May 1, the 798 men who had answered the call had been organized into 10 companies, which were sent east to help defend Washington, DC. Their arrival on May 17 was greatly cheered by the citizens of Washington, as the 1st Michigan was the first Western regiment to arrive in the capital.[1]

On July 21, the regiment participated in the first major battle, Bull Run, known to the Confederates as Manassas. The 1st Michigan fought as part of Heintzelman's division, and pressed the attack four times before being driven back under heavy fire. Their casualties were 6 men killed, 37 wounded, 70 missing, and 52 captured.[2]

The initial enlistment period of the soldiers in the 1st Michigan was set to expire in late July 1861, but the regiment was reorganized for a three-year enlistment on June 28. Additional men were drawn from all over the state, and their organization was completed at Ann Arbor. Command was given over to Colonel John O. Robinson, who held the post until April 1862, when he was appointed Brigadier General of Volunteers. After that, command passed to Lieutenant Colonel Horace S. Roberts.[3]

Chaplain Edwards, and probably his dog Bob, joined the regiment on October 31, 1861, after enlisting on August 17. As Edwards recalled in an essay written in 1886:

> *At first no law authorized my guild to go to the field,—as I have reason to know. I simply insisted upon going, to help care for scores to whom I had preached the gospel of armed castigation of rebellion. I confess to prompt unreasoning and perhaps unreasonable impulse toward the field. Enough to say, I went; and until my service ended—with proper definition—I enjoyed every*

*hour in a department that yielded to my regiment fifteen historic battles.*[4]

By the end of April 1862, the chaplain and Bob were well integrated into the regiment, and if the testimony of Lieutenant (later Captain) William Byrns is any indication, Bob was quite popular. In a letter to his lady friend, Florence Clark, dated "April the last, 1862," Byrns mourns his enforced idleness at Camp Butler in Newport News, and expresses his delight at encountering old Bob:

*Who is Bob? He is the grandest specimen of the canine race you ever saw. He is large and good natured. I seem to feel that in such weather he had better keep at a distance from his fair weather friends. Bob belongs to Chaplain Edwards but is at home with any of the officers. He cannot be coaxed from the Regiment. We have had him nearly six months. It is a very strange fact that he will not notice a private soldier or noncommissioned officer. Though true, but with all the "shoulder straps" he is very familiar and will follow any who call him. I took him to my tent and tried to get him into a frolic but he evidently has the rheumatism and will only play "shake hands" and look good natured. In despair I plunge beneath the blankets again and with Bob on the foot of my bunk go to sleep.*[5]

Byrns' letter to Florence, whom he later married,[6] is the only known reference to Bob, which makes him an unsung canine hero of the Civil War.

At the time of Byrns' letter, the 1st Michigan Infantry was attached to the Army of the Potomac, and supported General McClellan in the Peninsula Campaign of 1862. As part of the Fifth Corps, the 1st Michigan participated gallantly in the battles of Mechanicsville, Gaines' Mill, Peach Orchard, Savage's Station, Turkey Bend, White Oak Swamp and Malvern Hill between June 17 and July 1. In the process, 35 men were killed and 97 listed as missing.[7]

On August 30, 1862, they stepped into Hell itself at Manassas, Virginia, in the second major battle at that location. Shortly after 4 p.m., along with the 13th New York and 18th Massachusetts, the 1st Michigan was caught in crossfire, and suffered 50 percent casualties in minutes. The survivors withdrew and regrouped, but the regiment was badly mauled and unable to return to the front lines.[8]

Among those lost was the beloved Colonel Roberts, who had commanded them for just a year and a half. Chaplain Edwards served as the historian for the grisly battle:

*The regiment deployed column and with cheers advanced towards the enemy, our right resting near the railroad embankment, the center and left near a stone wall and railroad cut, in each of which places was posted a rebel battery. On our right and front was a force of the enemy's infantry, and as we advanced the regiment was subjected to a murderous fire from infantry and a cross-fire from five rebel batteries. The regiment suffered severely in crossing the open space. Colonel Roberts fell at an early moment after it deployed out of the woods. Four captains and three lieutenants—Captains Charles E. Wendell, Russell H. Alcott, Eben T. Whittlesey, Edward Pomeroy, and Lieutenants H. Clay Arnold, J. L. Garrison, and W. Bloodgood—met their death, and more than fifty per cent of the regiment were either killed or wounded.*

*Colonel Roberts was an active, efficient, brave, beloved, and is now a sincerely lamented leader. Captains Wendell, Alcott, Whittlesey, Pomeroy, and Lieutenants Arnold, Garrison, and Bloodgood were excellent officers, whose loss will be felt by the regiment, and mourned by their personal acquaintances.*

*The regiment went into battle with twenty officers and two hundred and twenty-seven men. Of the former but four are in camp unhurt, and of the latter hardly one hundred and fifty. In the action the 1st was placed in the center. In front was a rebel battery, and so destructive was its fire and so commanding its position, that General Porter ordered our brigade (Martindale's, of Morrill's division) forward to capture it. The service was so desperate, and so very sure were our officers of the death that awaited them, that they shook hands with each other in farewell. Like heroes they pressed on to the charge, until, coming within range, the enemy opened four additional batteries, hitherto masked, and poured in a deadly fire. Thus they were exposed to a cross-fire from five batteries at short range, throwing grape and canister, and to a flank fire of infantry. The result may be easily seen. Men fell like grain in harvest. Colonel Roberts was shot in the breast by a minie ball, and lived about ten minutes His words were, 'I am killed; tell Captain _____ to take command of the regiment.' He seemed to feel that he was about to fall, for previous to his going to his place in the line, he called me aside, and, after leaving some private messages, said: 'I trust that Michigan will believe that I tried to do my duty.'*[9]

Reverend Edwards remained the chaplain of the 1st Michigan until after the battle of Gettysburg (July 1-3, 1863), at which point he became an officer of the regiment. By the end of the war, Edwards had achieved the brevet rank of Colonel. He kept no other official records of the exploits of the 1st Michigan, but did end up becoming a significant literary figure. After the war, he served as assistant editor of Chicago's *Northwestern Christian Advocate*, eventually becoming its editor, a post he held until his death in 1901.

History does not record what became of friendly old Bob, but, since the chaplain does not record the death of his steadfast companion, perhaps he accompanied the reverend back home.

**Brigadier General Napoleon Bonaparte McLaughlen and staff in July of 1865. McLaughlen is seated second from the right. The headquarters servant sits on the ground with a small dog between his legs.** *(Courtesy of the Library of Congress)*

# Chapter 15

## Harvey and the Barking Dog Regiment

The 104th Ohio Volunteer Infantry, known as the regiment that captured the most Confederate battle flags in a single fight (11), was also known as the Barking Dog Regiment. During the three years of the regiment's existence, at least three dogs were among its ranks: Harvey, Colonel, and Teaser.[1] A fourth dog, known affectionately as "the blue pup," is mentioned, but he was apparently lost in a train accident sometime after his owner's death, Lieutenant James E. Williamson, in August 1863.[2]

But this wasn't the full extent of the 104th's corps of animal volunteers. On February 14, 1864, Captain William Jordan of Company K wrote home to his children describing the various pets accumulated by the regiment. Harvey and Colonel were described as veteran soldier dogs that go in any of the tents that they want and lay down at night or stand with the sentinels on guard. Lieutenant Colonel Oscar Sterl was the proud owner of a pet squirrel which had the run of the camp and would even "nibble at the ears" of Harvey and Colonel. Teaser, not knowing of the squirrel's status as pet, charged and was stopped only by the intervention of Harvey, who carefully grabbed the squirrel in his mouth and carried it to safety. Captain Jordan reported that the rescue proved unavailing, as the squirrel died of fright shortly afterwards. Additional animals in the 104th's menagerie included two raccoons and another squirrel that was kept secured by a tiny chain.[3]

The men of the 104th Ohio were recruited almost exclusively from the northeast parts of the Buckeye State in the summer of 1862, with the town of Wellsville providing the core of what became Company F.[4] One of the Wellsville volunteers was Daniel M. Stearns, a 29-year-old who had previously attained the rank of Lieutenant in Pennsylvania's 8th Reserve Regiment. When he joined Company F, Stearns brought with him Old Harvey, a veteran dog who had accompanied him during his previous stint on the battlefield and who had been wounded once in Virginia during the Peninsula Campaign. Harvey was a handsome Bull Terrier who resembled RCA's famous mascot named Nipper. Nipper was introduced to the world in 1898.

When Harvey's owner was promoted to 2nd Lieutenant in November 1862, Stearns fitted Harvey with a special leather collar whose brass nameplate read, "I am Lieutenant D. M. Stearn's dog; whose dog are you?"[5]

**After the war the men of the 104th Ohio Infantry remembered their dog Harvey by having his photo on keepsake buttons. Buttons like this one were worn by the veterans at their reunions.** *(Courtesy of Marcus S. McLemore)*

Harvey and his canine compatriots performed valuable service by keeping up the spirits of their comrades in uniform. Like Teaser and Colonel, Harvey wandered where he would and slept in any tent he cared to, and the soldiers were fiercely protective of him.[6] While the "blue pup" was famous for his tricks with fire, Harvey was a music lover.

**Harvey (lower left corner) relaxes with the regimental band of the 104th Ohio Infantry.** *(Courtesy of Marcus S. McLemore)*

On November 18, 1864, Private Adam Weaver of Company I wrote to his brother in Ohio that Old Harvey had paid him a visit while on picket. Weaver speculated that perhaps he smelled more like a dog than the boys of Company F. He also recounted that during the soldiers' campfire singalongs, Harvey would bark and move side to side. Weaver explained, "[M]y idea is that the noise hurts his ears, as it does mine!"[7] One surviving photo shows Harvey posing with the regimental band.

The year 1864 proved to be the 104th Ohio's most challenging year. After a bitter winter at Strawberry Plains near Knoxville, Tennessee, in the spring, they were sent to Cleveland, Tennessee, where troops were assembling preparatory for what would be the Atlanta Campaign. They participated in all of the campaign's general engagements.[8] May 13 found the Ohio boys at Resaca, Georgia, where their corps clashed with rebel troops under the command of General Joseph E. Johnston. Because the 104th was serving as reserves to the main brigade, their casualties were minimal: just 11 wounded, and one four-legged soldier. Harvey was wounded, but the extent of his injuries was not recorded. [9]

The 104th Ohio served with distinction at the battle of Utoy Creek on August 6, where they suffered over 30 casualties. Two days later, a second attack at Utoy Creek cost them a dozen more casualties.[10]

The 104th Ohio's severest test came at Franklin, Tennessee, in late November 1864. On the 30th they dug in at Franklin, constructing sturdy breastworks that served them well later that day. According to Nelson Pinney, a Private in the 104th Ohio:

> We took all the rails we could find and with them built a low-post and rail fence, outside of which we threw up an embankment deep and strong enough to protect us from the rebel shot and shell, with salient angles for cross firing and embrasures for the artillery. This was finished by two o'clock in the afternoon, when the boys, too tired to get dinner, lay down behind their new made works and lunched on crackers and raw bacon. For half an hour we rested, when brisk firing in front admonished us that we were not alone; and soon pell mell back the cavalry came, past the outer line, past the main line, through town, across the river. Through the woods came the rebel column, and filing off to the right and left in plain view they presented one of the grandest pageants we had ever beheld as regiments, brigades and divisions

*marched out and formed in line, with colors flying, to the*
*blare of trumpet and the rattle of drum, with all the pomp*
*and circumstance of glorious war.*[11]

All hell broke loose soon after, as General John Bell Hood's Confederates fell upon the entrenched Union troops. Historian Whitelaw Reid describes the battle of Franklin thus:

> *This was the most severe engagement the regiment had ever participated in, and its loss was sixty killed and wounded. Lieutenant William Kimball of company C, and Captain Bard of company I were killed in this battle. The men went into the fight with the avowed intention of revenging the loss of their comrades at Utoy Creek, and used that as their battle-cry. The Rebel General Adams was killed in front of the breastworks occupied by the One Hundred and Fourth Ohio, himself and horse rolling over in front of the regiment. Lieutenant Kimball, who lost his life, fought desperately, throwing hatchets and axes into the seething mass of Rebels in his front, until a bullet struck him down. Lieutenant Cope was severely wounded through the arm during the battle, but wrapping his handkerchief around the wound, bravely stood his ground throughout the battle. Lieutenant Coughlin, belonging to the staff of General Cox, was killed near the regiment while in the act of cheering his men.*
>
> *After the battle the regiment marched with the National forces to Nashville, bearing with it eleven battle-flags captured from the enemy.*[12]

In addition to securing 11 battle flags, a record for any regiment on either side of the struggle, the 104th and 100th Ohio regiments captured 1,100 Confederate prisoners that day.[13] Six of the 104th's later received the Medal of Honor for their valor at Franklin. Harvey was not one of those honored, but he surely served his regiment bravely during the battle.

Soon after Franklin the regiment participated in the battle of Nashville, where Lieutenant Stearns, Harvey's owner served as aide to Brigadier General James Reilly, and suffered a grievous injury.[14] Presumably, Harvey was with him, though he isn't mentioned in any documents. Once Hood's troops had been vanquished, the 104th Ohio transferred to North Carolina, where they engaged in several skirmishes. They remained there until the war's end, performing provost duty and receiving the arms and stores of Johnston's army after his surrender on April 26, 1865. In June 1865, they traveled to Camp Taylor near Cleveland, Ohio, where they received pay and were mustered out of the service.[15] Lieutenant Stearns ended his duty as Captain of Company F.

Sadly, Stearns passed away in an insane asylum in 1890.[16] Nothing is known of Harvey's fate after he mustered out, but years later, his memory was still held dear by the veterans of the regiment. His image adorns the face of their reunion badges, and a large oil portrait was painted in his honor. It is proudly displayed in a regimental reunion photo, 1886, by which time Harvey could only have been alive in memory.

"Harvey," Lieutenant Daniel M. Stearn's dog, 104th Ohio Infantry. This carte de visite, by Vick's Studio, Alliance, Ohio, is most likely a wartime image. However, it could have been taken at the time of the first annual reunion of the 104th Ohio, held in Alliance, Ohio, in November 1868. *(U. S. Army Military History Institute. rg98s)*

This photograph of the 17th annual reunion of the 104th Ohio Infantry was taken on the steps of the Lake Park Hotel at the Meyers Lake resort near Canton, Ohio in August, 1886. It shows the veterans of the 104th Ohio and their families, posing on the porch of the hotel. The veterans of the regiment chipped in to have a portrait painted of their regimental dog "Old Harvey"–a fellow veteran they would never forget. *(Meyers Lake Park, The Last Dance, Courtesy of Raymond Fete)*

**"Harvey", Lieutenant Daniel M. Stearn's dog, 104th Ohio Infantry.** *(U. S. Army Military History Institute. rg98s)*

# Chapter 16

## An Officer and a Canine

The Regiment that eventually became the 29th Maine Infantry began as a three-month enlistment as the 1st Maine Infantry. They formed on April 18, 1861, served in the defense of Washington, DC, then mustered out August 5. Most of the soldiers in the regiment came together again in October as the 10th Maine Infantry for two years of service, which expired in November 1863, at which point they were transferred into the 29th Maine Infantry.

One of the soldiers who managed to stay with the 1st, 10th, and 29th Maine Infantry for most of its lifespan was a furry fellow known as Major. While his origin remains shrouded in mystery, he exemplified the best of American military tradition. He was brave, reckless, encouraging, and ultimately gave his life in support of his comrades. That he had four legs rather than two, and was more apt to bark than yell his battle cry, made him no less a soldier. Major was a dark-haired, long-nosed mutt who served as the unofficial mascot of first Company H, and, later, of the entire regiment, from its first organization in Portland in April 1861, until his untimely death in the Red River Campaign of mid-1864. The "old dog," as he was called, was a favorite of the men and their enthusiastic supporter in battle.

In its first incarnation as the 1st Maine, the regiment saw little action. It wasn't sent into harm's way until, as the 10th Maine Infantry Regiment, it went south to Baltimore and then to Harper's Ferry, Virginia. The 10th Maine mostly performed guard duty in various locations until they were moved into the Shenandoah Valley in mid-May 1862. They engaged the Confederates at Winchester, Virginia on May 25, before their subsequent retreat to Williamsport, Maryland. On August 9, they participated in the battle of Cedar Mountain, Virginia.[1]

Shortly thereafter, the 10th Maine's mettle was tested in the infamous battle known as Antietam in the North. On September 15, George B. McClellan's Twelfth Corps of the Army of Potomac, of which the 10th Maine Infantry was then a part, and Robert E. Lee's Army of Northern Virginia had established clear battle lines on either side of Antietam Creek near the town of Sharpsburg, Maryland. Some 87,000 Union soldiers faced 45,000 determined Confederates. The battle commenced at dawn on September 17 and quickly evolved into an inconclusive bloodbath in which more men were killed and wounded than on any other day of the war and in all of American history. By late afternoon, when the fighting had ended, Federal casualties stood at 12,401, while the Confederate losses were 10,318.[2] Erhard Futterer, a member of the 20th New York State Militia, described what he saw when his company came across the 10th Maine at the battle of Antietam:

> *[W]e crossed the Antietam Creek and proceeded toward the East Woods where the 10th Maine Regiment, which had been reduced to a squad, was prostrate on the ground at the edge of the woods .... It was a panorama of the field of battle, which lay before us; the carnage of the fighting, which had raged since early morning, was everywhere: bodies of men, dead and wounded; wagons and barns burned; artillery pieces smashed; men running in confusion; and cornfields soaked in blood.[3]*

The 10th Maine acquitted itself well in the battle, losing 21 men killed, 50 wounded, and one missing. They had entered the battle with 277 officers and men in the ranks.[4] Perhaps the most disheartening loss was General Joseph K. F. Mansfield, a grizzled Mexican War veteran. With white beard and hair, he was vigorous and determined, and well regarded by his men for his veteran style. He was mortally wounded, however, when he received bad intelligence from a member of General Joseph Hooker's staff, and dashed along the 10th Maine's battle line on his horse, insisting they were firing on Union troops. He was soon convinced otherwise, but was wounded squarely in the chest before he could get to safety. He clung to life through the night, and died the next day.[5]

Major was in the thick of things, growling and barking, snapping at minie balls in flight. According to Major John Mead Gould, who helped the wounded Mansfield from the battlefield and later wrote a history of his regiment:

> *Old dog "Major" behaved well under fire, barking fiercely, and keeping up a steady growl from the time we went in till we came out. He had thus contributed his part towards the uproar which some consider so essential in battle. He had shown so much genuine pluck, moreover, that the men of [Company] H were bragging of his barking, and of his biting at the sounds of the bullets, asserting besides that he was "tail up" all day.[6]*

John Mead Gould was an inveterate journal writer, filling at least 16 large quarto volumes during his lifetime. His history of the regiment was based on his personal journals and diaries, and is extremely detailed. [7]

After Antietam, the 10th Maine participated in many of the well-known battles of the Civil War, but none was quite as devastating for them as Antietam. After passing through the carnage of Chancellorsville and Gettysburg, the soldiers of the 10th Maine served provost duty at the 12th Army headquarters until November 1863. At that point, the 10th was disbanded and its members transferred to the 29th Maine Infantry Regiment. By then, they had lost 82 men to the battlefield and 54 to disease. [8]

In March 1864, the 29th Maine joined the Nineteenth Corps in the Department of the Gulf and was sent on the Red River Campaign. On April 8, 1864, the 29th Maine and the rest of the Red River Expeditionary Force encountered the Confederates at Sabine Cross Roads, Louisiana, also known as the battle of Mansfield or Pleasant Grove. Old Major was particularly brave and active; dashing about the battlefield ahead of the front line, and that was his undoing. Gould noted emotionally in his regimental history:

*A word about our dog "Major" must be inserted. He was always a dog of singular behavior, but never acted so strangely as in his last fight. While in camp at the saw mill he was much disturbed at hearing the sound of the battle, and appeared to know that we should have to, or ought to go to the front. He barked wildly at every cavalry-man we met on the march—he seemed to know a straggler and skulk, and knew, too, that it was safe to bark at them. We never shall forget his actions at the top of the hill where we fought. As before stated, we came at that point upon almost a solid mass of fugitives, and here, too, we first heard the bullets whistle. The dog seemed to comprehend the situation, and bracing himself against the torrent, he gave one long, loud howl that rose above all other sounds, and then went on again. He ran wildly around the field, always keeping in our front, and biting at the little clouds of dust raised by the enemy's balls. At our first volley he jumped into the air, howled and bit at the flying bullets, and was going through strange capers when the fatal bullet struck him. He died like a hero, far in the front of the line, and had he been human we should not have felt his loss more keenly.*[9]

Mead notes in his journal that Major's death "cast a gloom over the whole regiment just as when one of the best and most loved of officers are killed."[10]

The men of the 29th Maine Infantry Regiment fought on without Major, participating in several smaller battles on the Red River Expedition before heading back north. After war's end, they served in Washington, DC, until June 1, performing provost duty during the Grand Review of the Army, May 23-24, 1865. Afterward, they served in various posts in South Carolina until they were mustered out at Hilton Head on June 21, 1866.[11] During their service as the 29th Maine, they had lost 42 men and one beloved dog in battle.

**General Rufus Ingalls with his horse and dog at City Point, Virginia, in March 1865. Ingalls was the chief quartermaster of all armies operating against Richmond on General Grant's staff starting in June 1864.** *(Courtesy of the Library of Congress)*

# Chapter 17

## Rover and the 44<sup>th</sup> New York

Too often, the flame of the ordinary person is lost in the glare of greater lights. Only in recent decades have historians turned their attention to the unsung heroes whose names may be on a long-forgotten casualty list or a line in a dusty census. Even more obscure are the stories of dogs that performed valiant duty on the front lines of a terrible war. For every well-documented Sallie of the 11<sup>th</sup> Pennsylvania Infantry or Stonewall Jackson of the Richmond Howitzer, there must be dozens of unsung canine soldiers who served their owners during the American Civil War, offering much needed amusement and support to the men of their units. Rover, the mascot of the 44<sup>th</sup> New York Regiment, was one such animal. The only evidence of Rover's existence is a photographic carte de visite, taken at the J. H. Abbott Studio in Albany, New York.

The 44<sup>th</sup> New York Regiment, popularly known as Ellsworth's Avengers, was organized in Albany in the autumn of 1861. The full name of the Regiment was the 44<sup>th</sup> New York Volunteer Infantry, the People's Ellsworth Regiment.[1] It was intended as a memorial regiment for the man it honored, Colonel Elmer Ellsworth, the first Union officer killed in the Civil War. Ellsworth was a friend of President Lincoln, the founder of the Zouave movement in America, and a well-respected young military officer who was killed in Alexandria, Virginia, by a southern hotel proprietor after removing a rebel flag from the hotel roof of his establishment.

Ellsworth's Avengers had some stringent membership requirements, at least in the beginning. The men had to be unmarried, able-bodied, younger than 30, of good moral character, not less than five feet, eight inches tall, and with some military experience. Obviously, this narrowed the field, and it appears that later in the war some requirements were loosened. The intention was for each town and ward in the area to provide one soldier as its representative, along with $100, gathered through subscriptions, to arm and equip him. Eventually, the subscription fee was lowered to $20, and each town and ward was allowed to contribute more than one solder. As a result, when they left Albany in October, the regiment was composed of 1,061 tall young men of superlative "character, intelligence, temperance, and morality."[2]

It was quite a while before the 44<sup>th</sup> New York saw much in the way of significant fighting. On May 27, 1862, the Avengers participated in the battle of Hanover Court House. The regiment performed bravely, with 30 men killed and 400 wounded, before the Confederates retreated. In the process, the regimental flag was pierced by more than 40 balls and was shot down 4 times.[3]

The heavy action continued, with the 44<sup>th</sup> participating in the battle of Gaines' Mills on June 27 and the battle of Malvern Hill on July 1, suffering significant casualties. Their leader, Colonel James C. Rice, held his regiment together under withering fire and charged the Confederates, capturing their flag and taking many of the rebels captive. Later, the men of the 44<sup>th</sup> served at the Second battle of Bull Run, where their numbers were reduced to 87 muskets strong.[4]

After being reinforced with new Albany recruits, the 44<sup>th</sup> New York saw additional action at Fredericksburg and Chancellorsville. On July 2, 1863,they held the extreme left of the Union line on a rocky knoll known as Little Round Top at Gettysburg, Pennsylvania, where they suffered 111 casualties. Later, in May 1864, the 44<sup>th</sup> New York accompanied the rest of the Army of the Potomac across the Rapidan River and fought at the Wilderness and Spotsylvania, losing half of its effective force during 11 days of continuous fire.[5]

The remaining men of the 44<sup>th</sup> New York forged on through the summer of 1864. By September 29<sup>th</sup>, they were back in Albany, numbering just 484 men, all that was left of the 1,061 men that had originally left Albany three years before, and the 700 additional men that reinforced them.[6] Those who hadn't yet fulfilled their terms of service were transferred to the 140<sup>th</sup> and 146<sup>th</sup> New York Infantry, along with the three-year survivors who wished to remain in service.[7]

And what of Rover, the mascot of the 44<sup>th</sup> New York?

Private James Woodworth mentions his own dog Rover in several letters, but it's uncertain whether this Rover was the Rover of the 44<sup>th</sup>. Woodworth's dog Rover comes to light in November 1862, when Woodworth received word that his wife Phoebe had broken her ankle when jumping from a runaway wagon. (Wartime necessity had prompted the Avengers to recruit married men by then.) Woodworth's horse, Old Foot, had been spooked by their dog Rover. In a letter dated November 13, 1862, he wrote to Phoebe:

*Dear Wife ... How is your ankle this morning. Does it pain to you very much or it is better, can't you walk the least bit. What made you jump out of the wagon while that Old Foot was running. I wish he had another kink in his back for being so hateful or was the dogs to blame, probably, they were you know I have always predicted that Rover would commit some dreadful act before he paid the last penalty for all living dogs. Poor luckless dog I wish he would show to the world that he was possessed of some intellect be it was so little. But I feel that what few brains he might have had were dryied up as rather burned up last summer while he was lying under the stove in The Shantie. If so he certainly is not to be unsured for his heedlessness.*[8]

It is possible that Private Woodworth removed Rover from his farmstead to protect his wife from further harm, pressing him into service with the regiment after Woodworth returned home for a short visit in 1863.

Woodworth's fate, at least, is known. In March 1864, he became one of the regiment's eight color bearers, and on May 8, he was killed near Spotsylvania Court House. Phoebe Woodworth apparently lived out her life on the income of a Civil War widow; she still had not remarried as late as 1883. His son Frankie, who was only two when James left home, grew up to serve four years as mayor of Bay City, Michigan.[9]

113

Written on the back of this carte de visite is "Rover 44th N.Y.S.V."
The image was taken by J. H. Abbott, 480 Broadway, Albany,
NY. An exact copy of this image can be found in the Orsell
Brown Papers Collection at the New York State Library in
Albany, New York. Orsell C. Brown served with the 44th New
York Infantry from 1861 to 1864. *(Author's Collection)*

This pre-war picture of William Smith, a private in the 44th New York Infantry, and his dog was sent by Smith with some of his personal information to Eugene Nash after the war. Nash, who was promoted in the 44th New York from private to captain, later authored a history of the regiment. Here is the information that Smith provided to Nash:

*Fayetteville, N. Y., August 9, 1910. "Will send you this picture which was taken just before enlisting. William Smith, private of Capt. Alien's Company F, 44th N. Y. Volunteers, enrolled on the 20th day of September, 1861 at Albany. N. Y., to serve three years. At the second battle of Bull Run was shot through the left ankle and taken prisoner. Myself and others were left on the battlefield eight days, by a stream of water with nothing to eat. We were then paroled and private carriages came from Washington. D. C., and took us to the U. S. Hospital, Judiciary Square. I was discharged January 7, 1863". ~~WM. SMITH. (A History of the Forty-fourth New York Infantry in the Civil War, 1861-1865, 1910)*

CDV portrait of a boy seated, brass-buttoned jacket, plaid pants, hat in lap, holding his dog next to him, in sharp focus. In period ink on bottom "Putnam Webber." Reverse side has a period ink inscription: "Putnam Webber, Beverly, Mass. Taken 1862. Received at Newbern N.C. while doing provost duty July 10th 1862." This is a note apparently written by his bother Charles Henry Webber a Musician in the 23rd Massachusetts Infantry while serving with his regiment in Newbern, North Carolina, summer 1862. Putnam himself eventually joined up, serving in the 2nd Company of Massachusetts Unattached Infantry for a 100-day and then a 90 day stint in 1864 from May 3 to November 15, 1864. Putnam was born September 7, 1847. *(Author's Collection)*

# Chapter 18

## Confederate Dogs at Gettysburg

The three-day battle of Gettysburg, July 1-3, 1863, was pivotal to the outcome of the American Civil War. Both sides knew the importance this battle would have on the war, which helps explain why the fighting was so furious. A total of 172,000 men and almost 90,000 horses participated in the battle and almost 51,000 men became casualties, 23,000 Union, 28,000 Confederate. Some 11,000 men died, 26,000 were wounded and recovered to varying degrees, and 14,000 were captured or listed as missing in action.[1]

William W. Fulton of the 5th Alabama wrote that on the morning of July 1st it was his Battalion that led the advance and fired the first shots on the Confederate side at Gettysburg.[2] Fulton also recalled that the first Southern casualty was not one of the men, but rather a four legged pet of Company A, 5th Alabama. As the first shower of Union cavalry bullets swept through their advancing skirmish line, one struck the company's little dog:

*A little dog had taken up with our company and was a pet with the boys. He was the first fellow shot in the ranks in the first day's battle. He was an innocent bystander, a harmless on-looker, so to speak, with no concern either way as to which side should whip, yet he was the first struck in the shower of lead and his life surrendered in good cause of States Rights and Home Rule.* [3]

Gettysburg also represented a vast stage, where soldiers of both sides played out everything that was good and noble in the American character, as well as ignoble, distressing and disheartening. Two brave Confederate dogs were among the noble. One gave his life and was buried with honors by the Union general that his friends fought against.

One of the more famous Civil War canines was immortalized in the painting "Repulse of General Johnson's Division by Geary's White Star Division"[4] by the noted 19th century artist Peter F. Rothermel. Little else is known about this brave dog, not even his name. In fact, it was more than a decade after Gettysburg that the mascot of the 1st Maryland Infantry (Confederate) became recorded into history.

Painting this battlefield scene in 1868, Rothermel depicted the dog as black and small to medium in size, but it's uncertain whether this rendering was based on reality or merely artistic license. Like most border states, Maryland's population was torn along factional lines, and regiments were organized for both the Union and Confederate causes. The 1st Maryland (Confederate) was organized in Winchester, Virginia, in summer 1861, and in its first incarnation consisted of some 600 men[5] and at least one dog.

In June 1863, the seven companies of the 1st Maryland joined Robert E. Lee's Army of Northern Virginia in his push to take the war to the North. The Marylanders marched into Pennsylvania and arrived at Gettysburg on the evening of July 1, too late in the day to participate in the fighting. They massed north of Culp's Hill and prepared for the battle as part of Brigadier General George H. Steuart's Brigade.

On the night of July 2, Steuart's Brigade captured and occupied a line of breastworks on Culp's Hill that had been constructed by Union troops. The next morning the brigade was ordered to renew the attack on Culp's Hill, but before the order was given, the men of the 1st Maryland already knew that they were being put into a desperate situation. Their objective was to take the Union line of earthworks that lay about 200 yards away on the other side of an open field.

Realizing the hopelessness of the task, Captain William H. Murray, who led Company A, 1st Maryland, shook the hand of every man in the company before the assault began, saying, "Good-bye, it is not likely that we shall meet again." As they charged into the open Pardee Field on Culp's Hill, they came under crossfire from both Union muskets and cannon. Despite the unrelenting Union fire, Captain Murray continued to lead Company A closer and closer to the enemy works until he was mortally wounded. As his brother Alex rushed to catch the falling William, he was struck by an exploding shell and knocked unconscious. A third brother, Lieutenant Clapham Murray, then assumed command of the Murray Company.[6]

By the time the survivors of the ill-fated charge withdrew to the safety of a stone wall they had captured the night before, the Marylander's had lost almost half its men, and other regiments of the brigade had suffered similar casualties.[7]

One of the Union officers, the colorful Brigadier General Thomas L. Kane, serves as the single primary source for information about the mascot of the 1st Maryland. During the blistering heat and confusion of July 3, Steuart's troops began advancing on Kane's position. As he watched Steuart's men move forward, Kane admired their steady advance and the redressing of their lines as men went down. Finally, the Confederate line wavered, and the survivors charged the Union lines. At that point, a dog dashed from the Confederate line and actually crossed into the Union formation. Kane described the action more than a decade later:

> A pet dog belonging to a company of the 1st Maryland (Confederate) charged with the regiment, ran ahead of them when their progress was arrested, and came in among the Boys in Blue as if he supposed they were what in better days they might have been, merely the men of another noisy hose or engine company, competing for precedence with his masters in the smoke of a burning building. At first—some of my men said, he barked in valorous glee; but I myself first saw him on three legs between our own and the Men in Gray on the ground as though looking for a dead master, or seeking on which side he might find an explanation of the Tragedy he witnessed, intelligible to his canine apprehension. He licked someone's hand, they said, after he was perfectly riddled.
>
> Regarding him as the only Christian-minded being on either side, I ordered him to be honorably buried.[8]

When Rothermel painted his famous scene in 1874, he put the mascot of the 1st Maryland in the thick of the action, based on eyewitness accounts.

The 1st Maryland fought on without their mascot, seeing action at Cold Harbor and in the trenches at Petersburg before surrendering at Appomattox. On that day, just three officers and 59 men received paroles, barely a tenth of the number of men the regiment had started with in 1861.[9]

* * *

Sawbuck was a more fortunate Confederate canine than the nameless dog of the 1st Maryland. The medium size, black-and-white bird dog was wounded once, but lived to see the end of the war. He served with the Louisiana Brigade of Stonewall Jackson's old division in the Army of Northern Virginia, under the command of Brigadier General LeRoy Augustus Stafford. Stafford, formerly the sheriff of Rapides Parish, Louisiana, was himself an unusual character. He had argued against secession, and once Louisiana joined the Confederacy, was initially unwilling to join the cause. This abruptly changed when he learned of a rumor that he didn't have the guts to fight. Outraged, he formed Stafford's Guards, which headed east on June 4, 1861. It later became Company B of the 9th Louisiana Infantry Regiment. They arrived at the battle of First Manassas just in time to miss the action, to their bitter disappointment. It wasn't until spring 1862 that Company B saw action, by which time Stafford had been promoted to Colonel in command of the entire 9th Louisiana.[10]

At Gettysburg, the battle in which Sawbuck's unnamed Maryland counterpart was killed on Culp's Hill, Stafford's men fought on a hill just to the west, Cemetery Hill, where the determined Louisianans briefly took the Union position during the twilight of July 2.

No one recounts which battles Sawbuck participated in, but it's known he was still serving after Stafford was promoted to Brigadier General in October 1863. A letter by John O. Casler appeared in Confederate Veteran Magazine March, 1913. Casler, who wrote about his own war experiences in *Four Years in the Stonewall Brigade,* recorded the following of Sawbuck:

> *I was greatly interested some time ago by an article in the Veteran about a dog* [Charlie Troup Artillery of Georgia] *that went through the war with Carlton's Battery and was killed at Appomattox* [actually Cumberland Church].
>
> *I knew of another soldier dog. This one was called "Sawbuck" by his master, and he was the special pet and mascot of the Louisiana Brigade in Jackson's old division, 2nd Corps, A. N. V. called the 4th, or Stafford's, Brigade. Sawbuck was a bird dog of medium size and with black and white spots. He always went into battle with the boys, and would run up and down the lines watching the fight. At last, however, he was wounded in the fore leg, and after that he remained in the rear when the firing was going on. He knew nearly every member of the brigade; and often in the evening, when the division was going into camp and he happened to be lost, he would stand by the road and watch the stragglers, and as soon as one of his own brigade came by he would follow him into camp.*[11]

In May 1864, General Stafford's luck ran out. One who had not wanted to fight his fellow Americans died on May 5 during the first day of the dreadful battle of the Wilderness, when he was shot directing his men to regroup to a more advantageous position. His men went on to fight at Spotsylvania Court House, Cold Harbor, and at the Siege of Petersburg, before surrendering at Appomattox on April 9, 1865. Sawbuck's fate remains uncertain, though it seems likely that he, too, surrendered that day.

These are the Confederate dogs believed to be at the battle of Gettysburg: The dog of the 5th Alabama Battalion, Company A; the dog of the 1st Maryland Infantry; Charlie, Troup Artillery; Robert Lee of the Troup Artillery; Sawbuck, 4th Louisiana Brigade; and Stonewall Jackson, Richmond Howitzers.

**Unknown dog of the period.** *(Author's Collection)*

*Hallie Cooke*

Civil War CDV of a drummer boy with a large dog. The boy is certainly old enough to be an actual serving drummer with a regiment. The tired look and well worn sack coat are signs of real service. The back mark reads R. E. Weeks, Photographer, Sandusky, Ohio. *(Author's Collection)*

# Chapter 19

## Sallie, the War's Most Famous Canine

Females rarely fought openly during the Civil War, but Sallie Ann Jarrett became famous for doing so.

Sallie served with distinction in the 11th Pennsylvania Volunteer Infantry Regiment from 1861 until her death at Hatcher's Run, Virginia, just two months shy of the war's end. Often pregnant, she made no effort to hide her gender, and ministered to "her boys" when not engaged on the battlefield. It was said she hated three things: civilians, Democrats, and women. Of course, Sallie Ann Jarrett was a dog.

She was a handsome brindled Bull Terrier, possibly a Staffordshire, one of the breeds often referred to as a Pit Bull. Despite their fearsome reputation, pit bulls tend to be loving and nurturing animals. In fact, the Staffordshire Terrier is often called "The Nanny Dog" in Britain. Sallie herself was fiercely loyal, brave in battle, and well loved by her comrades, who wrote stories, articles and poetry about her for many years after the war. She is the heroine of no less than three books, and when the regimental monument was erected at Gettysburg in 1890, her boys included a memorial to her. Therefore, more is known about Sallie than any other canine who participated in the Civil War.

The 11th Pennsylvania Infantry was organized for its three month service at Camp Curtin, near Harrisburg, Pennsylvania, April 26, 1861. Within days, they moved by rail to Camp Wayne, near the town of West Chester. The regiment consisted of young farmers, coal miners and lumbermen drawn from nine counties in south and west Pennsylvania.[1] These were rugged men who soon became some of the best fighters the Union had to offer. Among them was a Mexican War veteran, Captain Richard Coulter, who was quickly promoted to Lieutenant Colonel. Coulter, who later became the regiment's leader and Colonel, was among the first to write about Sallie. Coulter's story of Sallie first appeared in the *Republican and Democrat* of Greensburg, Pennsylvania, in 1867.

Sallie was mustered into service by the men of the regiment in May 1861, when she was barely four weeks old. She grew up surrounded by the bustle and strain of wartime service, and never knew another kind of life. Coulter explains how she came to be a part of the 11th Pennsylvania:

*One bright morning, a civilian, carrying on his arm a*
*small market basket, came to Capt. Terry's quarters, (Co. I)*
*enquired for him, and stated that he had brought him the pup*
*he had promised him; producing at the same time from the*
*basket, a little, puffy, pug-nosed, black-muzzled canine, scare*
*four weeks old, and barely able to toddle upon its short and*
*clumsy legs. The pup was taken into the quarters; a nest*
*provided for it under the Captain's bunk.*[2]

They named Sallie in honor of a favorite young lady of West
Chester and Phaon Jarrett, the regiment's first Colonel.[3] Sallie soon
found herself a favorite of the regiment and was promoted to
regimental mascot. Life in the camp during the 11th Pennsylvania's
training at Camp Wayne was easy for Sallie. Milk and soft bread
were plentiful and her days consisted of eating and sleeping. Captain
William Terry of Company I made a bed for her under his bunk.
While her new friends were being drilled in soldering, she spent her
time rolled up lazily on her blankets. She never lacked for attention
when they were free. Popularity did not spoil Sallie, however; she
was a respectful puppy, easy to get along with, never filching other
soldiers' food. In fact, she never touched anyone's rations unless they
were offered to her. When fresh beef was being issued, she would
stand without begging until she received her fair share. She would
even stretch out among haversacks full of meat without molesting
them, although that may have been due to an incident Coulter
described:

*"Sallie" was observed very suddenly to fall, roll over,*
*stretch her limbs, her body to tremble with a convulsion, and*
*she to give every appearance of speedy dissolution. All*
*thought that the dog experiment had proved a failure, and that*
*"Sallie" was dying. Nature, however, came to the rescue, and*
*after a gasp and struggle or two, she revived, and happily*
*survived her first attempt to swallow a ration of fresh beef,*
*which had well might proved her last.*[4]

Shortly thereafter Sallie narrowly escaped death again as she
accompanied her boys to their first assignment, guarding the rail
routes to Washington, DC. This marked the beginning of Sallie's
travels with the army. She traveled first-class in the arms of a soldier,
in a haversack, or rolled up in a blanket. Sometimes she rode on the

baggage wagon. At other times she was transported in the saddlebags of Dr. James Anawalt, the assistant regimental surgeon. She was even known to ride on the back of Richard Coulter's saddle.[5]

On one occasion during the maiden journey, Sallie was tied in a feed box on a baggage wagon as it forded the Potomac River. Shortly after crossing, a sharp jolt of the wagon caused her to fall out, and she was left choking at the end of a rope too short to reach to the ground. A quick-thinking soldier saved her life by cutting her down.[6]

Sallie formed a special attachment to a soldier who called himself the "Dageroon." Officially, Dageroon was a baggage guard, but everyone knew his real job was to take care of Sallie. He was a colorful character, and when the regiment passed through Philadelphia, he was weighted down by a variety of arms and supplies, leading Sallie along on a piece of twine, stopping occasionally so she could have a drink at a puddle or hydrant. When the regiment marched through the streets of Baltimore with loaded muskets at the half cock, Dageroon and Sallie again drew the curious attention of local residents as they walked together.[7]

The 11th Pennsylvania Volunteer Infantry first saw action as part of General Robert Patterson's division at the battle of Falling Waters, West Virginia, also known as Hoke's Run, on July 2, 1861. The Pennsylvanians faced the troops of two officers who would become heroes of the Confederacy: Cavalry leader Lieutenant Colonel J. E. B. Stuart, and Brigadier General Thomas J. Jackson, who would later earn the nickname "Stonewall." The result was a Union victory, primarily because Jackson had been ordered only to delay the Union advance. The Pennsylvanians acquitted themselves well and, though casualties were light on both sides, the first Pennsylvanian to die in the war was one of theirs.[8] They also suffered 10 men wounded.

On July 31, 1861, the regiment was mustered out of the service in Harrisburg, Pennsylvania; their three-month enlistment had expired. However, the 11th Pennsylvania was admired for its fighting ability, and the Union needed men like these. As early as July 19, steps were taken to re-organize the regiment under the same designation as a three-year regiment, and they became the first Pennsylvania regiment to re-enlist for three years' service.[9] Thus, as soon as they reached Camp Curtin and were mustered out, the men were mustered in again. On the recommendation of Colonel Jarrett, Richard Coulter was promoted to full Colonel and placed in charge of the regiment.[10] A soldier of the 12th Massachusetts Infantry Regiment, with whom the 11th Pennsylvania was brigaded in the winter of 1861, called Coulter "one of the greatest men I ever knew," and noted that Sallie had become known as "Dick Coulter's dog" by then.[11]

During the wait in Harrisburg, Sallie was stolen by a soldier of another unit. No one knew where she'd gone, despite her popularity; she would probably have been dismissed simply as "missing" had it not been for the Dageroon, who took enough time to scour the entire camp until he found her, whereupon he persuaded the thief to give her back. Though he never said how, it was rumored that the persuasion was both verbal and physical. Sallie then left on furlough with the men of the original Company I. She stayed at and visited the homes of several soldiers in Greensburg, Pennsylvania, until they re-organized, but she never saw her friend and protector again. When the soldiers returned to Camp Curtin, it was learned that the Dageroon had decided to join another regiment and had been killed in a train accident along the way.[12]

The regiment wintered in Annapolis, Maryland, and by spring 1862, Sallie was nearly full grown. Coulter describes her as a medium-sized dog, squarely but handsomely built, with a broad, deep chest and silky coat; her bright hazel eyes were full of "fire and intelligence."[13] It's said that she was frightened of civilians, always seeking the company of her soldiers when she encountered them. Later, she reacted much the same way when she encountered Confederates.

The men of the 12th Massachusetts also took notice of Sallie's personality. One soldier recoded this:

> Sally ... joined heartily in all the frolics of the soldiers and her temporal well-being was the constant care of a thousand men, as brave and true as any who ever went forth to battle at their country's call. In course of time the Eleventh found itself on the upper Potomac and we men of the Twelfth Massachusetts always regarded ourselves as fortunate in being brigaded with it.
>
> Sallie's acquaintances now became a great deal more numerous. Whether she took, in any degree, her characteristics from her owners and protectors, I never knew [why], but certain it was that at first she was just a little shy of us Massachusetts men. After a while, however, she consented to receive our attentions, and was always sure of a dainty breakfast from any Massachusetts tent into which she poked her nose—that is, if we were not worse off than dog's ourselves.[14]

**"Sallie" is perhaps the most famous Civil War canine. This photo was used as a model for the monument of the 11<sup>th</sup> Pennsylvania Infantry at Gettysburg, Pennsylvania.** *(Courtesy of the Pennsylvania Historical and Museum Commission, Pennsylvania State Archives, Record Group 218)*

The 11<sup>th</sup> Pennsylvania Monument was sculpted by E. A. Kretschman. The veterans of the 11<sup>th</sup> dedicated it to the "heroic dead" on September 3, 1890, and it stands on Oak Ridge on the Gettysburg Battlefield. The monument features a soldier preparing to fire. On the front of the base is a small bronze sculpture of Sallie, amidst the wounded, the dying and the dead, maintaining a silent vigil over her friends. *(Pennsylvania Gettysburg Battlefield Commission, Pennsylvania at Gettysburg: Ceremonies at the Dedication of the Monuments Erected by the Commonwealth. Vol. 1. Harrisburg, PA: Wm. S. Ray, 1914)*

Sallie soon became famous as a "soldier's soldier." With her regiment she learned the activities of soldering. She knew the drum and bugle calls, was the first one up at reveille, and usually attended morning roll call. At squad or company drill, she tended to pick a soldier and follow him patiently until drill was over. For regimental and brigade drill, Sallie took the lead and escorted Colonel Coulter's horse to the drill ground and remained in front of the horse until the troops were dismissed. During dress parade, she sought out the color sergeant and, during parade rest, lay down in the shade of the regimental colors.

A soldier from the 12th Massachusetts further wrote:

> *Many a time at dress parade did I go over to the camp of the Eleventh to see the important part that Sally always took in that imposing pageant. Then with the long line at "Parade rest," the drum corps slowly marching down the front, the Colonel with folded arms calmly looking into the faces of the men, and Sallie lying still at the feet of the color-bearer, as if she loved to be in the shadow of the flag, the scene was an impressive one. She seemed to understand for what purpose we were gathered there in that strange fashion and men who were not at all superstitious asserted it was their belief that the poor brute was in full sympathy with us in our loyal feeling.... On the march Sally followed closely behind the Colonel.... When the brigade came into camp the Eleventh was always sure of being represented by a Colonel, a flag and dog.[15]*

Sallie's respect for the colors at parade rest was sure to have been greatly admired by any Civil War solider. Her two self-assigned duties at Annapolis, to lead off with the colonel's horse as the regiment moved, and her place in front of the line at dress parade, were executed faithfully by her until the day she led the regiment into battle from their camp at Hatcher's Run.[16]

Four times during the war, Sallie carried out her duties while pregnant, up to a point. On March 7, 1862, she didn't show up for drill, and was later discovered nursing nine puppies in the hollow of the Liberty Tree on the St. John's College campus, Annapolis, Maryland. The Liberty Tree had been a meeting place for local patriots during the Revolutionary War period. The news of Sallie's first litter was announced at headquarters and an entry was made in the *Consolidated Morning Report Book* of March 7, 1862: "Sallie had a litter—nine pups."[17]

Two days later, however, Sallie was back on duty, her regimental callings overriding her maternal ones. When they were old enough, the pups were divided among the soldiers and shipped back home.[18] The 11th Pennsylvania was ordered to Washington, DC, on April 9, 1862, where they received new uniforms. Sallie got to meet President Lincoln on April 15, when the regiment was reviewed for the President's pleasure at the White House.[19] The regiment did not encounter the enemy until August 9, at the battle of Cedar Mountain were Sallie stood bravely under fire for the fist time. Regimental casualties were very light during the ensuing battle, only three men were wounded. Action was more or less continuous but light for the rest of that month, until Sallie and her boys came under fire at Thoroughfare Gap on August 28, losing 17 men killed and 40 wounded. Most of the casualties came from Company G, composed entirely of recruits who had just joined the regiment the day before.[20]

Two days later, they participated in the hard-fought battle of Second Bull Run. It was there that several of the regiment's color bearers were shot down. The regimental flag was saved but the national flag was captured. Colonel Coulter ended up in command of the brigade during the battle when the leader of the 12th Massachusetts, Colonel Fletcher Webster, was killed in action. Coulter escaped serious injury, but his horse, whom Sallie had led so many times to the parade ground, was shot in the neck and killed.[21] Sallie often took a position with the colors, not a particularly safe position, since several color bearers were shot down in battle.

Despite the confusion associated with large numbers of men in camp or on the march, Sallie always knew her own regiment. Even when thousands of troops passed by her, she never mistook the 11th for another regiment and never followed any other.[22] She was also happy to provide a little amusement for her boys. One popular camp story of Sallie was written by Richard Coulter in an 1867 pamphlet:

> *In pitching the camps at the end of a day's march, the rabbits were frequently started up from their hiding places, and then a scene took place, at once exciting and highly amusing. The poor rabbit, bewildered by the shouts of the men, would dash headlong, heedless of its course, "Sallie" close behind him, at the top of her speed, the men increasing in numbers as the chase progressed, over stacks of muskets, and piles of knapsacks and baggage, with shouts and cheers*

*and laugh, through shelter tents, stopping for nothing; the rabbit eluding many a vain grasp to seize him, and many a blow aimed at him with pick, shovel, musket or club, through the Regiment and Brigade, twisting, turning and doubling, until at length gaining the open field, he and "Sallie" would have a neck and neck race, out of which she always came the victor, and the unlucky rabbit furnished a grateful meal for the fleetest soldier . . . .*[23]

Then came the horrors of Antietam on September 17, 1862. Antietam was the bloodiest day of the entire Civil War, and some of that spilled blood belonged to the 11th Pennsylvania. Early in the battle, when entering the cornfield, their Brigadier General George Lucas Hartsuff was severely wounded. Colonel Coulter took command of the brigade as the battle intensified.

Sallie, for her part, decided to accompany one of the skirmishers into a cornfield. He tried to drive her back, fearing she would be killed, but she refused to leave the field, even when she was hit by a minie ball. The bullet merely grazed her side, literally "parting her hair." But she did not fall back until the rest of the regiment did, an exhausting four hours later. The soldier's concern for Sallie could have stemmed partly from the fact that she again was expecting puppies. [24]

A total of 27 men of the regiment were killed, with 89 more wounded and two captured. Sallie showed great sympathy for the wounded. One of the soldiers said that "Sallie came and licked their wounds." Her role that day had been not only to fight, but to comfort and make a dog's attempt to heal. [25]

A month later, the 11th Pennsylvania took part in the battle of Fredericksburg, where on December 13, the Army of the Potomac was badly beaten. The army took almost 13,000 casualties, more than twice as many as the Confederates, among them Colonel Coulter. He was severely wounded and carried from the field. Perhaps this unnerved Sallie, for she soon "advanced to the rear" at a rapid pace, crossed a pontoon bridge, taking refuge in a temporary hospital. Hours later the Union Army followed in her footsteps.[26] The regiment lost 15 men killed and 66 wounded that day.

Colonel Coulter later recovered from his wounds and returned to lead the regiment. During a review in April 1863, Sallie again met President Lincoln, and he doffed his signature stovepipe hat to her as she led the regiment past the review stand.[27] This recognition made the men of the regiment swell with pride.

Shortly afterward, the regiment was scheduled for a review with their division command. A soldier from the 12th Massachusetts tells of Sallie's experience at this review:

*The men were ordered to appear at their best. A certain Massachusetts regiment, well known throughout the army for its gallantry, resolved to outdo all others in cleanliness. So they visited all the sutlers and bought their entire stock of paper collars and white gloves, creating such a corner in the market that there were none left for the other regiments of the division. The review came. This regiment appeared, gorgeously adorned, their muskets shining in the sun, the men marching with heads erect and a firm tread born of a consciousness of superiority. Thus, the other less fortunate battalions were made to feel chagrined and unhappy. But the men of the 11th were not content to suffer without striking back, and just as the bands were playing "Hail to the Chief," with the reviewing officers and their staffs riding down in front, Sally appeared and followed along in front of the whole division, having a paper collar around her neck, and a white glove on each paw. The joke was good naturedly appreciated, and roars of laughter were heard long after the men broke ranks.[28]*

Soon after that, though no official explanation was offered, paper collars and white gloves were discontinued.[29]

Pennsylvanian George Gordon Meade commanded the Union army at the battle of Gettysburg, where for three unrelenting days, the Union Army of the Potomac and the Confederate Army of Northern Virginia battered each other in a fight that would prove to be the turning point of the War.

The 11th Pennsylvania joined the fight just before noon on the first day of the battle, July 1, as part of General Henry Baxter's brigade. They formed up behind Seminary Ridge near a railway embankment before being sent forward with the 97th New York to close a gap between the Union First and Eleventh Corps. As the two regiments moved forward, the New Yorkers and then Pennsylvanians engaged with enemy skirmishers. Hearing the battle intensify, Baxter sent the remainder of his brigade to join them at Oak Ridge.

Sallie's regiment took a position behind a stone wall on the left side of the brigade line, and soon engaged Brigadier General Alfred Iverson's North Carolinians. The Tar Heels advanced across an open field, having no idea that Baxter's brigade was concealed behind the stone wall, and that as many as 3,000 Union soldiers were about to open fire on them. At a distance of 80-100 yards, the Union commanders gave the order to "stand up and fire." The result was a devastating volley, thinning the Confederate ranks by more than 500 dead or wounded after the enfilade. Many others were so demoralized that they soon surrendered.

Surprisingly, General Iverson did not lead his men into the battle on that day. Iverson's brigade entered the battle with 1,400 strong North Carolinians. They suffered the highest percentage of loss of any Confederate brigade at the battle of Gettysburg.[30] Sallie and the 11th Pennsylvania were participates in what became known as the North Carolinian Sacrifice.

Despite their horrifying losses, the Confederates kept coming and soon outnumbered the Federals, pushing back both Union flanks. Sallie's regiment continued fighting on Oak Ridge for more than two hours, until ammunition ran low. At around 3:00 p.m., they were ordered back to the railway cut for re-supply and were later assigned to cover the Union retreat through the town. Casualties ran high among the Pennsylvanians that day, and they were forced to leave their dead and wounded behind. During a confused passage through to town of Gettysburg, Sallie was separated from her regiment, and the worst was feared. Meanwhile, her regiment went on to fight for two more days until the battle ended late in the day of July 3.

Sallie was not dead, however; she simply hadn't been willing to leave her fallen comrades at Oak Ridge. On July 5, as the last Confederates were leaving, Captain Benjamin F. Cook of the 12th Massachusetts found her there licking the wounds of her fallen comrades and holding faithful vigil among the dead of her regiment, starving and weak from the heat. She refused to leave the battlefield, however, until the wounded were carried to safety. Only then did she allow herself to be returned to her regiment to be nursed back to health. This was a show of loyalty and bravery that the men of the 11th Pennsylvania never forgot. [31]

On January 5, 1864, the three-year enlistment ran out for the men in the 11th Pennsylvania, and 204 men re-enlisted as veteran volunteers and received a 35-day furlough. Sallie made her second visit to Greensburg, Pennsylvania, for a well deserved rest.[32] The regiment soon reformed, 590 men and one dog strong.

In May, they participated in yet another horrific battle at the Wilderness, where an estimated 25,000 men were lost on both sides. Sallie's regiment engaged the Confederates late in the day on May 5.

In the course of that battle, which lasted well into the next day, they lost over one-third of their strength, 207 men killed and wounded.[33] Two days later, at the battle of Spotsylvania Court House against the veteran soldiers of Confederate General John B. Hood's division, Sallie was again struck by a minie ball; this one hit her in the neck and lodged there. Her wound was examined and temporarily bandaged by the field surgeon, who sent her with other wounded back to the hospital. There her wound was carefully reexamined by Dr. Chase, who pronounced that the wound was not dangerous, but the ball could not be removed; however, several months later, it came out on its own. She remained at the hospital for a short period of time recuperating before she rejoined the regiment. After returning to the regiment, her first notable performance was to tear out the seat of one soldier's pants as he broke ranks and retreated in panic through the line of the 11th.[34]

The 11th Pennsylvania got very little rest that year. They participated in several engagements after the Wilderness, including Cold Harbor, and the Siege of Petersburg. From May through winter, losses on the battlefields, skirmishes, on picket, and in the trenches totaled no less than 500 men for the 11th, though they continually received new recruits maintaining at least 200 members.[35] In December, they went on the mission to destroy of the Weldon Railroad. Richard Coulter remembered:

> *During the operations on the Weldon Road, the Hickford raid, and siege of Petersburg, she [Sallie] traveled along, or stayed with the men in the trenches or at the forts, or on the picket line, always at her old place at the head of the column when it moved, announcing the departure by barking and jumping at the horse of the officer in command, until the line fairly started, when she quietly trotted along, sometimes at the horses' heels, sometimes in the rear, or winding through the legs of the men in the middle of the column.*[36]

On the night of February 5, 1865, they camped near Hatcher's Run, Virginia. Sallie chose to sleep in the tent of Sergeant Benjamin F. Walker and three men of Company D, periodically waking them throughout the night with prolonged mournful cries. They sent her away several times, only to have her return and start howling again. Since this was not her normal behavior, she may have had a premonition of what was to come.

The next day Sallie led her regiment into battle, as usual, but it was for the last time. They engaged the Confederates at 2 p.m., and when the smoke cleared after the first volley, Sgt. Walker lay dead, along with another man from Company D with whom Sallie had bunked the night before. The other two men that shared the tent were severely wounded, and loyal Sallie, too, was dead. According to the regimental adjutant's official report of the battle:

> *"Sallie" was killed when the regiment was making its first advance upon the enemy the 6th instant, - she was in line with the file closers when shot. We buried her under enemy fire.*[37]

One of the soldiers in a letter dated "Camp near Hatcher's Run, Va., February 11, 1865," wrote:

> *Poor Sallie fell in the front line in the fight at the Run—a bullet pierced her brain. She was buried where she fell by some of the boys, even whilst under a murderous fire.*[38]

For the boys to have buried a dog while under fire, their love for that dog must have been equal to that for any of their fallen human comrades.

Sallie was no doubt sorely missed, but fortunately for the regiment's survivors, the war was nearly at an end. They saw only slight action until April 9 when Lee surrendered at Appomattox, little more than two months after Sallie was killed.

In 1890, the 11th Pennsylvania's regimental association erected a monument at Oak Ridge, in Gettysburg National Military Park. Atop a tall granite pedestal, the figure of a Union soldier stands, gun held upright, preparing to fire. Toward the bottom of the pedestal is a little ledge which bears the life-sized bronze figure of a stocky little dog lying quietly at vigil. Sallie was memorialized as a Civil War heroine, a representative of all other canine soldiers who gave their lives for their countrymen.

When the veterans of the 11th Pennsylvania Infantry erected their monument at Gettysburg in 1890, they included Sallie, the little dog who symbolizes deathless loyalty.

**An early war photograph of an overcoat-wearing Federal soldier from Company K, 11th Pennsylvania Reserves and dog.** *(Courtesy of Ronn Palm)*

Lieutenant Colonel Edgar Kimball of the 9<sup>th</sup> New York Infantry, Hawkin's Zouaves, and a faithful friend. Kimball was murdered by a fellow Federal officer, Brigadier General Michael Corcoran, on April 12, 1863, at Suffolk, Virginia. *(Courtesy of Scott D. Hann)*

**An oversized artillery officer with small dog.**
(Author's Collection)

GRANT IN PEACE.

**Civil War era CDV showing General Grant at Peace. Grant holds a little girl, possibly his daughter (Nellie). His dog lies next to the chair.** *(Author's Collection)*

Two views of General Rufus Ingall's dog. The top photograph was taken in March of 1865 on the steps of Appomattox Manor at City Point, Virginia, where General Grant and his staff made their headquarters. The bottom image does not have a given date. This may be the dog that Grant asked Ingall's if he expected to take it into Richmond with him and Ingalls replied "Yes . . . he belongs to a long-life breed." *(Courtesy of the Library of Congress)*

**This photograph taken by Timothy O'Sullivan in the fall of 1865 shows Company D, 188th Pennsylvania Infantry on Provost Guard duty at Appomattox Court House. Among the ranks of the company are two small dogs being held. The dogs squirmed during the photo and have lost some definition.** *(Courtesy of Appomattox Court House National Historical Park)*

# Glossary

**Adjutant** - A staff officer assisting the commanding officer, usually with correspondence and written orders.

**Battalion, Artillery** - An artillery battalion consisted of two or more battery units (a battery unit consisted of four to six cannon).

**Battalion, Infantry** - An organization containing less than 10 companies of men. Often contained from 4-8 companies.

**Battery** - The basic unit of artillery, consisting of four to six cannon, equivalent to a company in an infantry or cavalry regiment.

**Blockade runner** - A vessel, or its captain, specializing in evasion of the Union naval blockade of the South.

**Breastworks** - Temporary fortifications usually constructed of earth and or wood. They extended to breast or shoulder height.

**Brevet** - A promotion for conspicuous bravery or meritorious service. The promotion usually comes without an increase in pay and is often of an honorary (and temporary) nature.

**Brigade** - In the American Civil War, an operational unit consisting of two or more regiments. Two or more brigades were organized into a division.

**Canister shot (or canister)** - A type of artillery shell designed to explode upon firing, spraying out the lead or iron shot that was packed within the canister. It was a cruelly effective antipersonnel weapon, generally used at close range.

**Caisson** - A two-wheeled vehicle with large chests used for carrying artillery ammunition. Caissons were connected to a horse-drawn limber when moved.

**Company, infantry** - The basic operational unit in the Civil War-era army. A company was recruited to 100 officers and men.

**Corps** - In the American Civil War, an operational unit consisting of two or more divisions and commanded by a major general.

**Division** - In the American Civil War, an operational unit consisting of two or more brigades. Two or more divisions made up an army corps.

**Dress parade** - During the American Civil War dress parade was an everyday formal ceremony in which the troops were formed, assessed, reports of roll calls received, and important orders read. Weather permitting; the ceremony required that the soldiers to be in full dress uniform.

**Furlough** - A leave of absence granted to a soldier.

**Flank** - The right or left end of a military formation. Troops flanking an enemy must go around the far end, either on the right or left, of the enemy's position.

**Hardtack** - A durable cracker, or biscuit, made of plain flour and water and normally about three inches square and a half-inch thick.

**Haversack** - A canvas bag about one foot square, similar to a knapsack but worn over the shoulder. A soldier's bag used to carry rations, extra clothing, etc.

**Mustered** - To assemble. To be mustered in is to be enlisted or enrolled in service. To be mustered out is to be discharged from service, usually on expiration of a set time.

**Picket duty** - One or more soldiers on guard duty to protect their unit from surprise attack. During the Civil War, picket was another name for sentry.

**Provost duty** - A detail of soldiers acting as police under the supervision of an officer called a provost marshal.

**Regimental colors** - Each Civil War Infantry regiment had two flags; by military definition these were called the regimental colors—a national color and a regimental color.

**Regiments, infantry** - Regiments were formed from 10 companies of 100 men each. At full strength, Civil War Infantry regiments were normally comprised of 1,000 men each.

**Salient angles** - The portion of fortifications, line of defense, or systems of trenches that jut out toward enemy positions.

**Skirmishers** - Soldiers who are sent out in advance of the main body of troops to scout or probe the enemy position. The word also applies to soldiers who engage in a skirmish, or small fight.

**Solid shot** - A solid artillery projectile that is oblong or spherical, depending on whether the cannon it is fired from is rifled or smoothbore. Solid shot is primarily used against fortifications.

**Sutler** - A peddler with a permit to remain with troops in camp or in the field and sell food, drink, and other supplies.

**Volley** - In military parlance a volley is a simultaneous discharge of weapons, such as a volley of musket fire.

**A faithful dog remained by his owner until found by his comrades in this lithograph entitled "Recovered."** *(Courtesy of the Library of Congress)*

**Studio view of a Federal soldier with his dog.**
*(Author's Collection)*

# Appendix

## *Roster of the Loyal Hearts*

| Name & Regiment | Date Mustered Into Service By The Men | Remarks |
|---|---|---|
| **Bob** 1st Michigan Infantry (US) (Chaplin Edwards' dog) | Unknown | Served with the regiment during the Virginia Peninsula Campaign, Spring 1862. |
| **Candy** Co. B, 4th Texas Infantry (CS) | July 1861 | Separated from the regiment at Gaines' Mill, Virginia, June 27-28, 1862. Lost in the cornfield at Sharpsburg, Maryland, September 17, 1862 (reported captured). |
| **Charlie** The Troup Georgia Artillery (CS) | August 1, 1861 | Participated in 15 major engagements. Killed in action at Cumberland Church, near Farmville, Virginia, on April 7, 1865– two days before Lee's surrender. |
| **Curly** Co. A, 11th Ohio Infantry (US) | April 19, 1861 | Accidentally wounded on October 28, 1862. Became a prisoner but escaped at Chickamauga, Georgia, September 18-20, 1863. Suffered a broken foreleg after falling off a rail car near Bowling Green, Kentucky, June 1864. Died at age 12, and was buried at the National Soldiers Home in Dayton, Ohio. |

| | | |
|---|---|---|
| **Dash** 23rd Pennsylvania Infantry (US) | August 11, 1861 | Wounded several times and captured at Fair Oaks, Virginia, on May 31, 1862. Escaped capture on June 3, 1862. Honorably discharged, shipped by rail to Philadelphia, and lost en route, June 1862. |
| **Dog Jack** Co. A, 102nd Pennsylvania Infantry (US) | August 15, 1861 | Wounded at Malvern Hill, Virginia, July 1, 1862. Wounded (slight) at Fredericksburg, Virginia, Dec.13, 1862. Wounded (slight) at Marye's Heights May 3, 1863. Captured at Salem Church, Virginia, May 4, 1863, and exchanged as POW on October 20, 1863. Captured and escaped at Cedar Creek, Virginia, October 19, 1864. Disappeared at Frederick, Maryland, December 23, 1864. |
| **Frank** Co. B, 2nd Kentucky Infantry (CS) | August 1861 | Captured at Fort Donelson, Tennessee, Feb. 15, 1862, and paroled on August 26, 1862. Wounded numerous times during service. Disappeared in the summer of 1864. |
| **Harvey** Co. F, 104th Ohio Infantry (US) | August 9, 1862 | With the 8th Pennsylvania Reserves, he was wounded during the Virginia, Peninsula Campaign, spring/summer 1862, transferred with 1st Lt. D. M. Stearns into the 11th Ohio Infantry in August 1862. Wounded at Resaca, Georgia, May 14, 1864. |

| | | Mustered out with regiment, June 17, 1865. |
|---|---|---|
| **Jack** Co. A, 56th New York Infantry (US) "The Tenth Legion" | November 7, 1861 | The name Jack was inscribed on his silver collar. Wounded at Fair Oaks, Virginia, on May 31, 1862. Mustered out, October 17, 1865. Died of old age. |
| **Lieutenant Louis W. Pfeif's dog** Co. F, 58th Illinois Infantry (US) | December 31, 1861 | Pet of 2nd Lt. Louis Pfeif. Remained by Pfeif's body and his grave for 12 days at Shiloh, Tennessee, April 6 - 18, 1862. |
| **Major** Co. H, 10th & 29th Maine Infantry (US) | October 1861 | Killed in action at Sabine Cross Roads, Louisiana, April 6, 1864. |
| **Pet dog** of the 1st Maryland Infantry (CS) | Unknown | Killed in action at Gettysburg, Pennsylvania, July 3, 1863. |
| **Rover** 44th New York Infantry (US) | Unknown | Unknown |
| **Sallie** (Sallie Ann Jarrett) 11th Pennsylvania Infantry (US) | May 1861 | Bore four litters of puppies during service. Wounded slightly at Antietam, Maryland, September 17, 1862. Demoralized at Fredericksburg, Virginia, December 13, 1862. Separated from regiment at Gettysburg, July 1-5, 1863. Wounded at Spotsylvania Court House, Virginia, on May 8, 1864. Killed in action at Hatcher's Run, |

| | | |
|---|---|---|
| **Sawbuck**<br>4$^{th}$ Louisiana<br>Brigade<br>(CS) | Unknown | Virginia, February 6, 1865.<br>Special pet and mascot of<br>the 4$^{th}$ Louisiana Brigade.<br>Wounded in the foreleg–<br>location and date unknown. |
| **Sergeant**<br>3$^{rd}$ Louisiana<br>Infantry (CS) | July 1861 | Killed in action at Oak<br>Hills, Missouri, on August<br>10, 1861. |
| **Stonewall**<br>**Jackson**<br>Richmond<br>Howitzers<br>(CS) | Summer<br>1862 | Performed tricks in camp<br>taught to him by the<br>Howitzers. Believed stolen<br>by Louisiana Creole troops<br>later in the war. |
| **Tinker**<br>Confederate<br>Navy (CS) | 1862 | Served with Capt. M. P.<br>Usina while blockade<br>running. Buried at sea<br>(North Atlantic) in 1865,<br>shortly after war's end. |
| **Tony**<br>Battery A,<br>Illinois Light<br>Artillery<br>(US) | February<br>4, 1862 | Wounded at Fort Donelson,<br>February 15, 1862.<br>Wounded at Shiloh, April<br>6-7, 1862. Lost near<br>Larkinsville, Alabama, in<br>December 1863. |
| **Union Jack**<br>1$^{st}$ Maryland<br>Infantry (US) | May 1862 | Captured at Front Royal,<br>Virginia, on May 23, 1862.<br>Paroled on August 17,<br>1862. |
| **Washington**<br>**Pollock's**<br>**dog**<br>Co. H, 20$^{th}$<br>New York<br>State Militia<br>(US) | Unknown | Killed in action at<br>Antietam, Maryland, on<br>September 17, 1862. |

# Endnotes

*Chapter 1*

[1] William H. Tunnard, *A Southern Record: The History of the Third Regiment, Louisiana Infantry* (Baton Rouge, LA, 1866; reprint, Dayton, OH, 1970), 28.

[2] Ibid., 67.

[3] Shelby Foote, *The Civil War: A Narrative, Volume 1* (New York, 1958), 91.

[4] Tunnard, *A Southern Record*, 51.

[5] Ibid., 67.

[6] Ibid., 53.

*Chapter 2*

[1] Maryland. *Commission on the Publication of the Histories of the MD Volunteers During the CW. History and Roster of the Maryland Volunteers, War of 1861-5. Vol. 1* (Silver Spring, MD, 1987), 9.

[2] Charles Camper and J. W. Kirkley, comps., *Historical Record of the First Regiment Maryland Infantry, with an Appendix Containing a Register of the Officers and Enlisted Men, Biographies of the Deceased Officers, Etc. War of the Rebellion, 1861-65* (Baltimore, 1990; reprint of 1870 edition), 38.

[3] Ibid., 39.

[4] Ibid., 48.

[5] *Harper's Weekly*, November 8, 1862, "Union Jack: The Pet of Our Richmond Prisoners."

[6] Ibid.

[7] Ibid.

**Chapter 3**

[1] Foote, *The Civil War, Volume 2*, 21.

[2] Ibid., 22.

[3] Ibid., 44.

[4] Frank H. Taylor, *Philadelphia in the Civil War* (Philadelphia, 1913), 111.

[5] United States Censuses for 1860.

[6] *Saturday Evening Post*. December 27, 1862, "Fidelity of a Dog on the Battle-Field."

**Chapter 4**

[1] T. L. Steward, "Curly: A Military Dog." *From the 11th Infantry Proceedings of the ... Annual Reunion of the Eleventh Ohio Infantry.* (Various Publishers, 1869-1914), Second Annual Reunion, 28.

[2] *The Ohio Soldier*, May 5, 1888, T. L. Steward, "Curly's Civil War Record. History of a Dog Which Deserved a Pension from Uncle Sam."

[3] Joshua H. Horton, *A History of the Eleventh Regiment (Ohio Volunteer Infantry), Containing the Military Record, So Far as It is Possible to Obtain It, of Each Officer and Enlisted Man of the Command ... Compiled From the Official Records* (Dayton, OH, 1866), 246.

[4] *The Ohio Soldier*, Steward, "Curly's Civil War Record."

[5] Ibid.

[6] Ibid.

[7] Horton, *A History of the Eleventh Regiment*, 246-47.

[8] Steward, "Curly: A Military Dog," Second Annual Reunion, 30.

[9] Ibid., 23.

[10] Ibid., 30.

[11] *The Ohio Soldier*, Steward, "Curly's Civil War Record."

[12] Steward, "Curly: A Military Dog," Second Annual Reunion, 30.

[13] Margaret Kruckemeyer, RN. President, the American Veterans Heritage Center, Dayton, OH.

## Chapter 5

[1] Robert Stiles, *Four Years Under Marse Robert* (New York, 1903), 170-71.

[2] Ibid., 171

[3] Ernest L. Abel, "Faithful Friends." *Civil War Times Illustrated*. (April 1995), 48.

[4] Stiles, *Four Years*, 172.

[5] Carlton McCarthy, *Reminiscences of the First Company of Richmond Howitzers*. (Ann Arbor, MI: University Microfilms, 1972; reprint of earlier edition), 46-47.

[6] Val. C. Giles and Mary Lasswell, eds., *Rags and Hope: The Recollection of ... Four Years with Hood's Brigade, Fourth Texas Infantry, 1861-1865* (New York, 1961), 26.

[7] Donald. E. Everett, ed., *Chaplain Davis and Hood's Texas Brigade*. (San Antonio, 1962), 234

[8] Val C. Giles, *Brake Collection*, U. S. Army Military History Institute, Carlisle, PA.

[9] Everett, ed., *Chaplain Davis and Hood's Texas Brigade*, 234.

[10] Giles, *Brake Collection.*

[11] Stephen W. Sears *Landscape Turned Red: The Battle of Antietam,* (New York, 1983), 294-96.

[12] Giles, *Rags and Hope,* 279.

[13] Charles B. Kimbell, *History of Battery "A," First Illinois Light Artillery Volunteers* (Chicago, 1899), 80-82.

[14] Ibid., 81-82.

## Chapter 6

[1] United States Census for 1840.

[2] Will Plank, *Banners and Bugles: A Record of Ulster County, New York and the Mid-Hudson Region in the Civil War* (Marlborough, NY, 1972), 11-12.

[3] *The Baltimore American,* September 23, 1862, "The Battle of Sharpsburg; General McClellan and the Army; Incidents on the Field."

[4] Rufus R. Dawes *Service With the Sixth Wisconsin Volunteers.* (Dayton, OH, 1991 reprint of 1890 ed.), 92-93.

[5] Ibid., 93.

[6] Steven R. Stotelmyer, *The Bivouacs of the Dead* (Baltimore, 1992), 31.

## Chapter 7

[1] Michael P. Usina, "Blockade Running in Confederate Times," *The Confederate Veterans Association Newsletter,* July 4, 1893.

[2] Ibid.

[3] Ibid.

[4] Donald Booth, Jr., "Usina Family Articles Page" [online], *The Ancient City Genealogist*, Vol. VII, Issue 1, February 1996. [Cited 1 May 1, 2007]. Available from: http://www.menorcansociety.net/articles/usinapage.html.

[3] Usina, "Blockade Running in Confederate Times."

[4] Ibid.

[5] Ibid.

[6] Ibid.

[7] Ibid.

[8] Ibid.

[9] Ibid

### Chapter 8

[1] Will Plank, *Banners and Bugles: A Record of Ulster County, New York and the Mid-Hudson Region in the Civil War* (Marlborough, NY, 1972), 61.

[2] Joel C. Fisk and William H. D. A. Blake, *A Condensed History of the 56th Regiment New York Veteran Volunteer Infantry* (Newburgh, NY, 1906), 15.

[3] Amanda McGinnis and Cynthia Rapp, "'Our Name is Legion!' was the Proud Boast of the 56th New York Volunteers," *America's Civil War*, September 1990, 64.

[4] Ibid.

[5] Ibid., 65.

[6] Ibid., 66.

[7] Fisk, *A Condensed History of the 56th Regiment New York,* 15-16.

## Chapter 9

[1] Joseph H. Crute, Jr., *Units of the Confederate States Army.* (Midlothian, VA, 1987), 130.

[2] Edwin Porter Thompson. *History of the Orphan Brigade.* (Louisville, KY, 1898), 252-53.

[3] Ibid., 253.

[4] William C. Davis, *Diary of a Confederate Soldier* (Columbia, SC, 1990), 110.

[5] Thompson, *History of the Orphan Brigade,* 253.

[6] "Two Dogs." *The Bivouac, Volume 1* (1882-1883), Published Monthly by the Southern Historical Association of Louisville, KY, 72-73.

[7] Crute, *Units of the Confederate States Army,* 130.

## Chapter 10

[1] Foote, *The Civil War, Volume 1,* 350.

[2] 1860 U.S. Census Record on Louis W. Pfeif.

[3] *The Union Army A History of Military Affairs in the Loyal States 1861-65—Records of the Regiments in the Union Army—Cyclopedia of Battles—Memoirs of Commanders and Soldiers.* 8 Volumes (Madison, WI, Federal Publishing, 1908), Volume 3.

[4] Foote, *The Civil War, Volume 1,* 328.

[5] Ibid., 336.

[6] Ibid., 341.

[7] 1860 U. S. Census Record on Louis W. Pfeif.

[8] Frank Moore, *Civil War in Song and Story* (New York, 1889), 130.

**Chapter 11**

[1] Ed Rehn, *Diary* (Frank P Marrone Jr. 23<sup>rd</sup> Pennsylvania Re-enactors. http://www.23rdpa.com/)

[2] Ibid.

[3] William J. Wray, *Life of the 23<sup>rd</sup> Pennsylvania "Birney's Zouaves" Civil War* (William J. Wray: 1903; reissued by Lisa Wray Mazzanti, 1999, 2003), 18, 53.

[4] Ibid., 17.

[5] Ibid., 53.

[6] James G. Shinn, From the *23rd Inf. Regt. "Fair Oaks": Report of the First Annual Reunion of the Survivor's Association, 23d Penna. Vols.* Held at Männerchor Hall, Philadelphia, PA, May 31, 1882 (Philadelphia, 1883).

[7] Ibid.

[8] Ibid.

[9] Ibid.

[10] Rehn, *Diary*.

[11] Shinn, *23rd Inf. Regt. "Fair Oaks"*

[12] Rehn, *Diary*.

[13] Wray, *Life of the 23<sup>rd</sup> Pennsylvania*, 155-56.

[14] Shinn, *23rd Inf. Regt. "Fair Oaks"*

[1] John H. Niebaum, "History of the Pittsburgh Washington Infantry, 102nd (Old 13th Regiment)," *Pennsylvania Veteran Volunteers and Its Forbearers* (Pittsburgh, 1931), 116.

[2] Ibid.

[3] *American Civil War Society Newsletter,* June 1998, "Making Legends of Regimental Mascots."

[4] Niebaum, "History of the Pittsburgh Washington Infantry," 117.

[5] Alexander M. Stewart, *Camp, March and Battlefield of Three Years and a Half with the Army of the Potomac* (Philadelphia, 1865), 270-71.

[6] Ibid., 271.

[7] Niebaum, "History of the Pittsburgh Washington Infantry," 116-17.

[8] Stewart, *Camp, March and Battlefield*, 273.

[9] Ibid., 270-74.

[10] Niebaum, "History of the Pittsburgh Washington Infantry," 116.

[11] Ibid., 98.

[12] Ibid., 116.

[13] Ibid., 117.

[14] Ibid.

## Chapter 13

[1] George B. Atkisson and William S. Smedlund, eds., "Charlie 'Recruit' to Troup Artillery," *Confederate Veteran*, Volume 19 (1911), 515-16.

[2] William S. Smedlund, Brief History of the Troup Artillery. www.jackmasters.net/troup/index.html.

[3] Atkisson, "Charlie 'Recruit' to Troup Artillery," 515.

[4] Stiles, *Four Years Under Marse Robert*, 170-71.

[5] W. A. Hemphill, "The Troup Artillery," *Atlanta Constitution* (republished from Confederate Veteran, June 1899), 260.

[6] Atkisson, "Charlie 'Recruit' to Troup Artillery," 515-16.

## Chapter 14

[1] John Robertson, comp., *Michigan in the War* (Lansing, MI, 1880) 168.

[2] Ibid.

[3] Ibid., 169.

[4] Arthur Edwards, "Those Who Fought Without Guns," *Military Essays and Recollections* (MOLLUS, Volume 1, Chicago, 1891), 444.

[5] Byrns, William. Letter to Florence Clark, dated April 21, 1862.

[6] Historical Data Systems, comp. *American Civil War Soldiers* [database on-line], Provo, UT, 1999.

[7] Robertson, *Michigan in the War*, 169.

[8] Ibid.

[9] Ibid., 169-70.

**Chapter 15**

[1] Timothy Brookes, "'Harvey': War Dog of the 104th Ohio: A Biography from the Canine Corps," *Military Images Magazine* (March/April 1994), 19.

[2] Nelson A. Pinney, *History of the 104th Regiment Ohio Volunteer Infantry, 1862 to 1865* (Akron, OH, 1886), 129.

[3] Brookes, "'Harvey': War Dog of the 104th Ohio," 19.

[4] Pinney, *History of the 104th Regiment Ohio Volunteer Infantry, 1862 to 1865*, 129.

[5] Brookes, "'Harvey': War Dog of the 104th Ohio," 18.

[6] McLemore, Marcus S. Civil War collector and owner of McLemore's Canine Training and Kennel, Poland, OH.

[7] Brookes, "'Harvey': War Dog of the 104th Ohio"19.

[8] Reid, *Ohio in the War*, 563.

[9] Pinney, *History of the 104th Regiment Ohio*, 129.

[10] Ibid., 51.

[11] Ibid., 60.

[12] Reid, *Ohio in the War*, 563.

[13] Pinney, *History of the 104th Regiment Ohio*, 61.

[14] Brookes, "'Harvey': War Dog of the 104th Ohio,"19.

[15] Reid, *Ohio in the War*, 564.

[16] Brookes, "'Harvey': War Dog of the 104th Ohio" 19.

## Chapter 16

[1] Frederick H. Dyer, *A Compendium of the War of the Rebellion, Volume 2* (Dayton, OH, 1979 reprint), 1222.

[2] Sears, *Landscape Turned Red*, 294-96.

[3] C. Eugene Miller and Forrest F. Steinlage, *Der Turner Soldat: A Turner Soldier in the Civil War, Germany to Antietam* (Louisville, KY, 1988), 97.

[4] John M. Gould, *The Civil War Journals of John Mead Gould, 1861-1866* (Baltimore, 1997), 197.

[5] Sears, *Landscape Turned Red*, 206.

[6] John M. Gould, *History of the First-Tenth-Twenty-ninth Maine Regiment, in Service of the United States, From May 3, 1861, to June 21, 1866* (Portland, ME, 1871), 245.

[7] Gould, *The Civil War Journals of John Mead Gould*, preface.

[8] Dyer, *A Compendium of the War of the Rebellion. Vol. 2*, 1222.

[9] Gould, *History of the First-Tenth-Twenty-ninth Maine*, 419.

[10] Gould, *The Civil War Journals of John Mead Gould*, 326.

[11] Dyer, *A Compendium of the War of the Rebellion. Vol. 2*, 1222.

## Chapter 17

[1] Eugene A. Nash, *A History of the Forty-fourth New York Infantry in the Civil War, 1861-1865* (Dayton, OH, 1988; reprint of 1910 ed.), 6.

[2] Ibid., 6-12.

[3] F. W. Beers, *The History of Herkimer County, New York* (New York, 1879).

[4] Ibid.

[5] Ibid.

[6] Ibid.

[7] Frederick Phisterer (comp.), *New York in the War of the Rebellion*, (Albany, NY, 1912), 2,289.

[8] Christopher Hunter, *A Civil War Private: James Woodworth of the Forty-fourth New York Volunteer Infantry and the Family he Left Behind* (MA Thesis, SUNY-Albany, 2000).

[9] Ibid.

## Chapter 18

[1] Gary Kross (Licensed Battlefield Guide), *Stephen Recker's Virtual Gettysburg* (Sharpsburg, MD, 2002), 7-9.

[2] William F. Fulton, *The War Reminiscences of William Frierson Fulton II, 5th Alabama Battalion, Archer's Brigade, A. P. Hill's Light Division, A. N. V.* (Gaithersburg, MD, 1986), 77.

[3] Ibid., 79.

[4] Pennsylvania Historical and Museum Commission. The State Museum of Pennsylvania Art Collections 06.4.3.

[5] Crute, *Units of the Confederate States Army,* 161

[6] Daniel C. Toomey, *Marylanders at Gettysburg* (Baltimore, 1994), 24-25.

[7] Ibid., 28.

[8] Kane to Rothermel, March 21, 1874, Rothermel Papers, Pennsylvania State Archives.

[9] Crute, *Units of the Confederate States Army*, 162.

[10] Sons of Confederate Veterans Louisiana Division, cited  May 1, 2007, "General Leroy Augustus Stafford," available from: http://www.lascv.org/358.htm.

[11] John O. Casler, "Sawbuck, A Noted Dog In The Virginia Army." *Confederate* Veteran, Volume 21 (March, 1913), 139.

***Chapter 19***

[1] Cindy Stouffer and Shirley Cubbison, *A Colonel, a Flag and a Dog* (Gettysburg, PA, 1998), 10.

[2] Richard Coulter, Greensburg, PA, *Republican and Democrat* December 18, 1867 "Sallie," 1.

[3] John D. Lippy, Jr., *Sallie the War Dog* (Harrisburg, PA, 1962), 19.

[4] Coulter, "Sallie," 2.

[5] Stouffer, *A Colonel, a Flag and a Dog*, 11.

[6] Coulter, "Sallie," 2.

[7] Ibid.

[8] Stouffer, *A Colonel, a Flag and a Dog*, 13.

[9] Ibid., 17.

[10] Bates, Samuel P. *History of Pennsylvania Volunteers, 1861-5. Volume 1* (Harrisburg, 1869-1871), 247.

[11] "Soldiers' Faithful Dog, Sallie." *The Gettysburg Compiler.* October 19, 1910.

[12] Coulter, "Sallie," 3.

[13] Ibid.

[14] *The Gettysburg Compiler*, "Soldiers' Faithful Dog, Sallie."

[15] Ibid.

[16] Coulter, "Sallie," 3.

[17] Ibid.

[18] Ibid., 4.

[19] Stouffer, *A Colonel, a Flag and a Dog*, 24.

[20] Bates, *History of Pennsylvania Volunteers, 1861-5, Volume 1*, 251.

[21] Stouffer, *A Colonel, a Flag and a Dog*, 30.

[22] Coulter, "Sallie," 7.

[23] Ibid.

[24] Stouffer, *A Colonel, a Flag and a Dog*, 33.

[25] Ibid., 34.

[26] Coulter, "Sallie." *Republican and Democrat*, 4-5.

[27] Lippy, *Sallie the War Dog,* 31-32.

[28] *The Gettysburg Compiler*, "Soldiers' Faithful Dog, Sallie."

[29] Lippy, *Sallie the War Dog,* 31.

[30] Kross, *Stephen Recker's Virtual Gettysburg*, 24-25.

[31] Coulter, "Sallie," 5.

[32] Stouffer, *A Colonel, a Flag and a Dog*, 50.

[33] Bates, *History of Pennsylvania Volunteers, 1861-5. Vol. 1*, 261-262.

[34] Coulter, "Sallie," 6.

[35] Stouffer, *A Colonel, a Flag and a Dog*, 61.

[36] Coulter, "Sallie," 6.

[37] Ibid.

[38] Ibid.

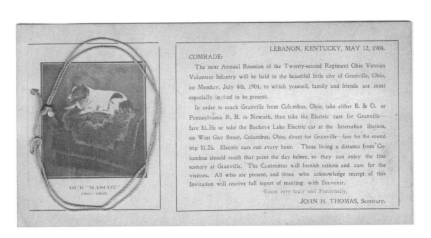

**The mascot of the 22nd Ohio Veteran Volunteer Infantry is featured on a 1904 unit reunion card. Attached to the card is a string with possibly some of the dog's hair affixed to it.** *(Courtesy of Marcus McLemore)*

An unidentified patriotic Federal officer with sword in hand and
his dog that appears worn out and ready for a nap. *(Courtesy of
Ronn Palm)*

# Bibliography

Abel, Ernest L. "Faithful Friends." *Civil War Times Illustrated.* April 1995.

Atkisson, George B. "Charlie 'Recruit' to Troup Artillery." *Confederate Veteran.* Volume 19, 1911.

Bates, Samuel P. *History of Pennsylvania Volunteers, 1861-5.* 5 Volumes. Harrisburg: State Printer, 1869-1871.

Beers, F. W. *The History of Herkimer County, New York.* New York: F. W. Beers & Co., 1879.

Booth, Jr. Donald. "Usina Family Articles Page" [online]. *The Ancient City Genealogist.* Volume VII, Issue 1 February 1996. [Cited 1 May 2007]. Available from: http://www.menorcansociety.net/articles/usinapage.html.

Brown, Liz. Interlibrary Loan Coordinator, Worcester County Library, Snow Hill, MD.

Brookes, Timothy. "'Harvey': War Dog of the 104th Ohio: A Biography from the Canine Corps." *Military Images Magazine* March/April 1994.

Camper, Charles, and Kirkley, J. W. comps. *Historical Record of the First Regiment Maryland Infantry, with an Appendix Containing a Register of the Officers and Enlisted Men, Biographies of the Deceased Officers, Etc. War of the Rebellion, 1861-65.* Baltimore: Butternut and Blue, 1990 (reprint of 1870 edition).

Casler, John O. "Sawbuck, A Noted Dog In The Virginia Army." *Confederate Veteran.* Vol.ume 21, March 1913.

Coulter, Richard. "Sallie." *Republican and Democrat.* Greensburg, PA, December 18, 1867.

Crute, Joseph H., Jr. *Units of the Confederate States Army.* Midlothian, VA: Derwent Books, 1987.

Dawes, Rufus R. *Service With the Sixth Wisconsin Volunteers.* Dayton, OH: Morningside, 1991; reprint of 1890 ed.

Davis, William C. *Diary of a Confederate Soldier: John S. Jackman of the Orphan Brigade.* Columbia, SC: University of South Carolina Press, 1990.

Dyer, Frederick H. *A Compendium of the War of the Rebellion. Volume 2.* Dayton, OH: Morningside, 1979.

Everett, Donald. E. ed. *Chaplain Davis and Hood's Texas Brigade.* San Antonio, Texas: Principia, 1962.

Fisk, Joel C., and Blake, William H. D. A. *A Condensed History of the 56th Regiment New York Veteran Volunteer Infantry.* Newburgh, NY: Journal Printing House, 1906.

"Fidelity of a Dog on the Battle-Field." *Saturday Evening Post.* December 27, 1862.

Foote, Shelby. *The Civil War: A Narrative, 3 Volumes.* New York: Random House, 1958.

Fulton, William F. *The War Reminiscences of William Frierson Fulton II, 5th Alabama Battalion, Archer's Brigade, A. P. Hill's Light Division, A. N. V.* Gaithersburg, MD: Butternut Press, 1986.

Giles, Val C. Brake Collection. U. S. Army Military History Institute, Carlisle, PA.

Giles, Val. C. and Mary Lasswell, eds. *Rags and Hope: The Recollection of ... Four Years with Hood's Brigade, Fourth Texas Infantry, 1861-1865.* New York: Coward-McCann, 1961.

Gould, John M. *History of the First-Tenth-Twenty-ninth Maine Regiment, in Service of the United States, From May 3, 1861, to June 21, 1866.* Portland, ME: Stephen Berry, 1871.

_____. The Civil War Journals of John Mead Gould, 1861-1866. Baltimore, MD: Butternut and Blue, 1997.

Hemphill, W. A. "The Troup Artillery." *Atlanta Constitution*, republished from Confederate Veteran, June 1899.

Horton, Joshua H. *A History of the Eleventh Regiment (Ohio Volunteer Infantry), Containing the Military Record, So Far as It is Possible to Obtain It, of Each Officer and Enlisted Man of the Command ... Compiled From the Official Records.* Dayton, OH: W. J. Shuey, 1866.

Hunter, Christopher. *A Civil War Private: James Woodworth of the Forty-fourth New York Volunteer Infantry and the Family he Left Behind.* MA Thesis, SUNY-Albany, 2000.

Kane to Rothermel, March 21, 1874, Rothermel Papers, Pennsylvania State Archives.

Kimbell, Charles B. *History of Battery "A," First Illinois Light Artillery Volunteers.* Chicago: Cushing, 1899.

Kross, Gary (Licensed Battlefield Guide). *Stephen Recker's Virtual Gettysburg.* Sharpsburg, MD: Another Software Miracle, 2002.

Kruckemeyer, Margaret. RN. President, the American Veterans Heritage Center, Dayton, Ohio.

Lippy, John D. Jr. *Sallie the War Dog.* Harrisburg, PA: Telegraph Press, 1962.

"Making Legends of Regimental Mascots," *American Civil War Society Newsletter*, June 1998.

Marrone, Frank P. Jr. 23$^{rd}$ Pennsylvania Re-enactors. http://www.23rdpa.com/

Maryland. *Comm on the Publication of the Histories of the MD Volunteers During the CW. History and Roster of the Maryland Volunteers, War of 1861-5. Volume 1.* Silver Spring, MD: Family Line Pubs., 1987.

McCarthy, Carlton. *Reminiscences of the First Company of Richmond Howitzers.* Ann Arbor, MI University Microfilms, 1972 (reprint of earlier edition).

McGinnis, Amanda, and Rapp, Cynthia. "'Our Name is Legion!' was the Proud Boast of the 56th New York Volunteers." *America's Civil War*, September 1990.

McLemore, Marcus S. Civil War collector and owner of McLemore's Canine Training and Kennel, Poland, OH.

Miller, C. Eugene, and Steinlage, Forrest F. *Der Turner Soldat: A Turner Soldier in the Civil War, Germany to Antietam.* Louisville, KY: Calmar Publications, 1988.

Moore, Frank. *Civil War in Song and Story.* New York: P. F. Collier, 1889.

Nash, Eugene A. *A History of the Forty-fourth New York Infantry in the Civil War, 1861-1865.* Dayton, OH: Morningside, 1988 reprint of 1910 ed.

Niebaum, John H. "History of the Pittsburgh Washington Infantry, 102nd (Old 13th Regiment)." *Pennsylvania Veteran Volunteers and Its Forbearers.* Pittsburgh: Burgum Print Co., 1931.

Palm, Ronn. Ronn Palm's Museum of Civil War Images, Gettysburg, PA.

Pennsylvania Historical and Museum Commission, Pennsylvania State Archives.

Pennsylvania Historical and Museum Commission. The State Museum of Pennsylvania Art Collections.

Peery, Charles V. MD, Charleston, South Carolina.

Phisterer, Frederick (comp.). *New York in the War of the Rebellion, 1861-1865.* Albany, NY: Weed and Parsons, 1912.

Pinney, Nelson A. *History of the 104th Regiment Ohio Volunteer Infantry, 1862 to l865.* Akron, OH: Werner & Lohmann, l886.

Plank, Will. *Banners and Bugles: A Record of Ulster County, New York and the Mid-Hudson Region in the Civil War.* Marlborough, New York: Centennial Press, 1972.

Reagin, Shawn. Berlin, Maryland. Eisighollen@aol.com.

Rehn, Ed. *Diary.* Frank P Marrone Jr. 23rd Pennsylvania Re-enactors. http://www.23rdpa.com/

Reid, Whitelaw. *Ohio in the War: Her Statesmen, Her Generals and Soldiers, 1861-1865.* Volume 2. Cincinnati, OH: Wilstach, Baldwin, 1872.

Sears, Stephen W. *Landscape Turned Red: The Battle of Antietam,* New York: Houghton Mifflin, 1983.

Shinn, James G. 23$^{rd}$ Inf. Regt. "Fair Oaks": Report of the First Annual Reunion of the Survivor's Association, 23d Penna. Vols. Held at Männerchor Hall, Philadelphia, Penna., May 31, 1882. Philadelphia: W. P. Kildare, l883.

Smedlund, William S. *Brief History of the Troup Artillery.* www.jackmasters.net/troup/index.html.

Sons of Confederate Veterans Louisiana Division. "General Leroy Augustus Stafford" [online cited 1 May 2007]. Available from: http://www.lascv.org/358.htm.

Stewart, Alexander M. *Camp, March and Battlefield of Three Years and a Half with the Army of the Potomac.* Philadelphia: J. G. Rodgers, 1865.

Steward, T. L. "Curly: A Military Dog." From the 11$^{th}$ Infantry Proceedings of the … Annual Reunion of the Eleventh Ohio Infantry … Various Publishers, 1869-1914.

_____. "Curly's Civil War Record. History of a Dog Which Deserved a Pension from Uncle Sam." *The Ohio Soldier.* May 5, 1888.

Stiles, Robert. *Four Years Under Marse Robert.* New York: Neale, 1903.

Stotelmyer, Steven R. *The Bivouacs of the Dead.* Baltimore, MD: Toomey Press, 1992.

Stouffer, Cindy, & Cubbison, Shirley. *A Colonel, a Flag and a Dog.* Gettysburg, PA: Thomas, 1998.

Taylor, Frank H. *Philadelphia in the Civil War.* Philadelphia: City of Philadelphia, 1913.

Toomey, Daniel C. *Marylanders at Gettysburg*. Baltimore, MD: Toomey Press, 1994.

"The Battle of Sharpsburg; General McClellan and the Army; Incidents on the Field." *The Baltimore American*, September 23, 1862.

*The Union Army A History of Military Affairs in the Loyal States 1861-65—Records of the Regiments in the Union Army —Cyclopedia of Battles—Memoirs of Commanders and Soldiers*. 8 Volumes. Madison: Federal Publishing, 1908.

Thompson, Edwin Porter. *History of the Orphan Brigade*. Louisville, Kentucky: Lewis N. Thompson, 1898.

Tunnard, William H. *A Southern Record: The History of the Third Regiment, Louisiana Infantry*. Baton Rouge, Louisiana: Printed for the Author, 1866; reprint, Dayton, Ohio: Morningside, 1970.

"Two Dogs." *The Bivouac, Volume 1*. 1882-1883, published monthly by the Southern Historical Association of Louisville, Kentucky.

"Union Jack: The Pet of Our Richmond Prisoners." *Harper's Weekly*. 8th November, 1862.

United States Census Records, 1840.

United States Census Records, 1850.

United States Census Records, 1860.

USAMHI - U.S. Army Military History Institute, U. S. Army History Collection, Carlisle Barracks, Pennsylvania.

Usina, Michael P. "Blockade Running in Confederate Times." *The Confederate Veterans Association Newsletter*, July 4, 1893.

Wray, William J. *Life of the 23rd Pennsylvania "Birney's Zouaves" Civil War*. William J. Wray: 1903; reissued by Lisa Wray Mazzanti, 1999, 2003.

# Index

**A Federal Artilleryman in a frockcoat with his dog.**
*(Courtesy of Marcus McLemore)*

# About the Author

Michael Zucchero attended Kent State University and is now a business manager with a regional supermarket chain, an industry in which he has more than 25 years' experience.

Mike was introduced into Civil War life during his childhood by his history-loving dad, Bill. Mike enthusiastically engaged in Living History events for more than fifteen years, portraying a Confederate infantryman at re-enactments in throughout the country.

For over a decade, Mike has been researching and collecting memorabilia on American Civil War canines and mascots. He is currently working on volume two in his series on dogs of the Civil War and would welcome other well documented stories to add to his collection.

A native of Ohio, Mike, his wife Tanya, and his dog Peanut Butter, live near Ocean City, Maryland.

For a complete book and price list write:

**SCHROEDER PUBLICATIONS**
**131 TANGLEWOOD DRIVE**
**LYNCHBURG, VA 24502**
www.civilwar-books.com
E-mail: civilwarbooks@yahoo.com
434-525-1865

Titles Available:
* **Thirty Myths About Lee's Surrender** by Patrick A. Schroeder
ISBN 1-889246-05-0

* **More Myths About Lee's Surrender** by Patrick A. Schroeder
ISBN 1-889246-01-8

* **The Confederate Cemetery at Appomattox** by Patrick A. Schroeder
ISBN 1-889246-11-5

* **Recollections & Reminiscences of Old Appomattox and Its People**
by George T. Peers ISBN 1-889246-12-3

* **Tar Heels: Five Points in the Record of North Carolina in the Great
War of 1861-5** by the Committee appointed by the North Carolina Literary
and Historical Society ISBN 1-889246-02-6 (Soft cover) ISBN 1-889246-
15-8 (Hard cover)

* **The Fighting Quakers** by A. J. H. Duganne ISBN 1-889246-03-4

* **A Duryée Zouave** by Thomas P. Southwick ISBN 1-561900-86-9 (Soft
cover) ISBN 1-889246-24-7 (Hard cover)

* **Civil War Soldier Life: In Camp and Battle** by George F. Williams
ISBN 1-889246-04-2

* **We Came To Fight: The History of the 5th New York
Veteran Volunteer Infantry, Duryée's Zouaves, (1863-1865)**
by Patrick A. Schroeder ISBN 1-889246-07-7

* **Campaigns of the 146th Regiment New York State Volunteers** by
Mary Genevie Green Brainard ISBN 1-889246-08-5

* **The Bloody 85th: The Letters of Milton McJunkin, A Western Pen-
sylvania Soldier in the Civil War** Edited by Richard A. Sauers, Ronn Palm,
and Patrick A. Schroeder ISBN 1-889246-13-1 (Soft cover) ISBN 1-
889246-16-6 (Hard cover)

* **The Highest Praise of Gallantry:  Memorials of David T. Jenkins & James E. Jenkins of the 146<sup>th</sup> New York Infantry & Oneida Cavalry** by A. Pierson Case (1889) with New Material by Patrick A. Schroeder
ISBN 1-889246-17-4

* **Where Duty Called Them:  The Story of the Samuel Babcock Family of Homer, New York in the Civil War** by Edmund Raus
ISBN 1-889246-49-2

* **The Opportunity Is At Hand:  Oneida County, New York, Colored Soldiers in the Civil War** by Donald M. Wisnoski  ISBN 1-880246-20-4 (Soft cover)  ISBN 1-889246-18-2 (Hard cover)

* **So You Want to Be a Soldier:  How to Get Started in Civil War Re-enacting** by Shaun C. Grenan  ISBN 1-889246-19-0

* **The Pennsylvania Bucktails:  A Photographic Album of the 42<sup>nd</sup>, 149<sup>th</sup>, 150<sup>th</sup> Pennsylvania Regiments** by Patrick A. Schroeder
ISBN 1-889246-14-X

* **A Summer on the Plains with Custer's 7<sup>th</sup> Cavalry:  The 1870 Diary of Annie Gibson Roberts** Edited by Brian C. Pohanka  ISBN 1-889246-21-2

* **The Life of Ely S. Parker:  The Last Grand Sachem of the Iroquois and General Grant's Military Secretary** by Arthur C. Parker
ISBN 1-889246-50-6 (Hard cover) ISBN 1-889246-52-2 (Leather bound limited edition)

* **"We Are Coming Father Abra'am" The History of the 9<sup>th</sup> Vermont Volunteer Infantry, 1862-1865** by Don Wickman  ISBN 1-889246-23-9

* **A Vermont Cavalryman in War and Love:  The Civil War Letters of Brevet Major General William Wells and Anna Richardson** Edited by Elliott W. Hoffman  ISBN 1-889246-51-4

* **While My Country is in Danger:  The Life and Letters of Lt. Col. Richard S. Thompson, 12<sup>th</sup> New Jersey Volunteers** by Gerry Harder Poriss & Ralph G. Poriss  ISBN 0-9622393-6-4

* **No Middle Ground:  Thomas Ward Osborn's Letters from Field (1862-1864)** Edited by H. S. Crumb & K. Dhalle  ISBN 0-9622393-4-8

* **Unfurl the Flags:  Remembrances of the American Civil War** Edited by W. E. Edmonston  ISBN 0-9622393-0-5

* Out of the Wilderness:  The Civil War Memoir of Corporal Norton C. **Shepard** Edited by Raymond W. Smith  ISBN 1-892059-00-2

* **A History of the 117th Regiment, New York Volunteers (Fourth Oneida)** by James A. Mowris  ISBN 0-9622393-8-0

* **The Telegraph Goes to War:  The Personal Diary of David Homer Bates, Lincoln's Telegraph Operator** Edited by Donald E. Markle

* **Shepherdstown:  Last Clash of the Antietam Campaign September 19–20, 1862** by Thomas McGrath  ISBN 1-889246-39-5

* **The Appomattox Campaign, March 29 – April 9, 1865** by Chris M. Calkins  ISBN 1-889246-55-7

* **Charlie's Civil War:  A Private's Trial by Fire in the 5th New York Volunteers, Duryée Zouaves, and the 146th New York Volunteer Infantry** Edited by Charles Brandegee Livingstone ISBN 1-889246-42-5

* **Sailor's Creek:  Major General G. W. Custis Lee, captured with controversy** by Frank Everett White, Jr.  ISBN 1-889246-56-6

Have your Civil War ancestors researched at the

National Archives.

Union or Confederate.

Military Service Records and Pension Records.